362.19   Banish, Roslyn,
BAN   1942-

         Focus on living.

                                    11BT03088

$24.95

US ON LIVING

DATE			

Focus on Living

PORTRAITS OF AMERICANS WITH HIV AND AIDS

Photographs and Interviews by ROSLYN BANISH

Introduction by Paul A. Volberding, M.D.

UNIVERSITY OF MASSACHUSETTS PRESS AMHERST AND BOSTON

Printed in China

LC 2002014512

ISBN 1-55849-394-8 (cloth); 395-6 (paper)

Designed by Kristina Kachele

Set in FFAtma Serif Book with Gill Sans Light display

Printed and bound by Everbest Printing Co., through Four Colour Imports, Ltd.

Library of Congress Cataloging-in-Publication Data

Banish, Roslyn

Focus on living : portraits of Americans with HIV and AIDS /

photographs and interviews by Roslyn Banish ; introduction by Paul A. Volberding

p. cm.

ISBN 1-55849-394-8 (cloth : alk. paper)—ISBN 1-55849-395-6 (pbk. : alk. paper)

1. AIDS (Disease)—Patients—United States—Interviews. 2. AIDS (Disease)—

Patients—United States—Portraits. I. Title.

RC606.54 .B36 2003

362.1′969792′00973—dc21   2002014512

British Library Cataloguing in Publication data are available.

In memory of my mother, Lillian Schlesinger Banish, 1910–2001,

an artist who embraced life, every minute of it

Contents

Acknowledgments

AT THE CORE of this work are the people who came forth to tell their stories and be photographed. My heartfelt thanks to all the individuals within these pages, as well as to those whose stories were not included in the final edit. Everybody was brave and generous and patient. Thank you!

Besides these volunteers, I met with a number of people whose input helped shape the course of the project. Many of them were connected to the AIDS community and were able to provide background information. Some of these individuals helped me recruit volunteers, one of the most challenging tasks. Thank you to the following individuals and organizations:

Linda Brandt, Rural AIDS Action Network, Minneapolis; Vince Crisostomo, Asian Pacific Wellness Center, San Francisco; Kelly Celony, Mt. Sinai Adolescent Health Center, New York City; Nancy Evans and Sanjai Rabab Moses, Center for Youth, San Francisco; Bruce Fisher, Huckleberry House, San

Francisco; Mick Gardner, Centerforce, San Rafael, California; Dr. Tricia Hellman Gibbs, San Francisco Free Clinic; Jeff Henne; Leo Joslin; Rachel Kesselman and Jody Reiss, Jewish Family and Children's Services, San Francisco; Jody Hurwitz; Susan Landor Keegin; Deborah Kent, AIDS Research Institute, University of California San Francisco; Barbara Klemm, Mt. Sinai Medical Center, New York City; Pamela Krasney; Nicole Livingston; Nicholas Metcalf, Minnesota Men of Color, Minneapolis; Larry Meredith, Department of Public Health, San Francisco; Bay Positives, San Francisco; Dr. Jim O'Donnell; Deborah Oppenheim, U.S. Department of Health and Human Services; Dick Pabich; Naomi Prohovnick, Lyon-Martin Women's Health Services, San Francisco; Thom Robbins, YMCA of San Francisco; Greg Schoonard, Central California Women's Facility, Chowchilla; Shanti, San Francisco; Dr. Lydia Temoshok, Institute of Human Virology, Baltimore; Shirley Selhub and Dr. Ann Webster, Mind/Body Medical Institute, Boston; Kelly Wallace, Marin AIDS Project; San Rafael, California; Shafia Zaloom.

The following friends, family, and colleagues have been more than helpful. They have been generous, loyal, and kind. Their support ranged from providing warm hospitality when I was photographing out of state to looking at the work in progress and sharing ideas and sensibilities. Some guided me through the most daunting task of all, funding and book publication. I am deeply grateful to all of my collaborators:

Sue Shoemaker Adams, Susan Coe Adams, Doris Adelstein, Nancy Adler, Freude Bartlett, Charlotte Burchard, Amelia Davis, Dr. Giff Boyce-Smith, Roy Eisenhardt, Andrew Epstein, Jennie Epstein, Paul A. Epstein, Sydney Goldstein, Kaatri Grigg, Jane Hart, Vivian Levitt, Kathleen Lynaugh, Terry Lorant, Arthur Martin, Eric Mosbrooker, Dr. Richard and Hoppie Penn, Paula Peterson, Kathy Pick, Toby Rosenblatt, Abby Sadin, Neal Sofman and Anna Bullard, Marion Spirn, Naomi Spirn, Gretchen Stone, Kina Sullivan, Lynn Twist, Barbara Wilson.

A critical piece of the project was funding. Paula Podesto Fracchia's commitment was huge. Her kind offer to find grant support allowed me to bring the project to completion. Barbara Kimport, Development Director, YMCA of San Francisco, generously shared her expertise. I am also grateful to Ann Hatch of the Clinton Walker Foundation, whose initial support launched my idea, and to Bean Finneran for her challenge grant which made completing the work possible. Additional and much-appreciated funding came from two anonymous donors and from Doris and Harvey Adelstein; Nancy Adler and Arnold Milstein; Seymour Banish; Myra Goodall Block; Julie Cheever and Fred Altshuler; Sandy and Joseph Cohen; Betsy and Roy Eisenhardt; Paul A. Epstein; Adriana Fracchia; Sydney Goldstein and Chuck Breyer; Kaatri and Doug Grigg; Carol A. Harris/Union Pacific Railroad Company; Phyllis Hattis Fine Arts, Inc; Susan B. Jordan; Barbara and David Kimport; Susan Korsower; Dr. Myles Lippe; LEF Foundation; Vivian and Richard Levitt; Molley and Richard Lowry; Jackie and John McMahan; Barbara and Richard Mendelsohn; Gail and Pat Murphy; Kristina and Owen O'Donnell; Payne Family Foundation; Kathy and Grant Pick; Margaret Z. Robson; Sally and Toby Rosenblatt; Alice Schaffer Smith; Marion and Irwin Spirn; Tin Man Fund; and Rae Victor.

My thanks to Dr. Paul A. Volberding for his introduction and to Bruce Wilcox, Director, University of Massachusetts Press.

Finally, I am grateful to Marin AIDS Project, San Rafael, for serving as fiscal agent for the project.

Thank you all.

R. B.

Preface

BEING A PARENT, one who on both a conscious and an unconscious level has entertained the possible dangers that could visit my children, all children, at any time, probably had a lot to do with my undertaking this project. I wanted the world to be a safer place.

In 1996 I attended a workshop at my children's high school. It featured a panel of four very winning young people who were living with AIDS. The panelists each had a unique story to tell. All spoke in a direct, no-nonsense way, describing how they contracted AIDS, how, upon diagnosis, their lives had suddenly changed forever. It took my breath away to learn about the day-to-day challenges facing them, their fears, their dreams. I was moved, not by the sadness of their stories, but by their bravery in the telling of their stories, and their resolve to continue living.

That evening I left the workshop with a new understanding about those living with AIDS. I wanted everyone to hear those stories and more. I knew that through photographs and interviews I could be the communicator. My first use of the photograph/interview format was for *City Families: Chicago and London* (Pantheon, 1976), which compared a cross-section of English and American families by giving them a platform—a photograph and an interview—from which to present themselves.

I set out to find people living with HIV/AIDS who were willing to be photographed and tell their stories. I would provide the platform. My aim was to include as diverse a group of individuals as possible—people of different sexual orientations, different ages, and from many ethnic and economic backgrounds. As one woman told me: "This is the ultimate nondiscriminatory virus. It doesn't care what color your skin is, it doesn't care how much money your mommy makes, where you live, how old you are."

My first volunteers came through agencies and nonprofit organizations that serve people with AIDS. Some of the people I photographed and interviewed for the project referred me to their friends as possible participants. For an organization to be helpful in recruiting volunteers, it took at least one exceptional person who would go out of the way to speak to clients on my behalf. For example, at New York's Mt. Sinai Adolescent Health Center, social worker Kelly Celony took great care and much time discussing my project with her adolescent group, fielding their concerns and questions, relaying my responses. At San Francisco's Center for Youth, executive director Nancy Evans and her associate Sanjai Rabab Moses enthusiastically embraced my efforts. It is committed people like Kelly, Nancy, and Sanjai who made this book possible.

Once volunteers came forth, I would try to set up an appointment. My preference for a meeting venue was their place of residence, if they had one, which afforded privacy as well as visual variety for the photography. Because it was not always possible to meet where they lived, we also got together in flourescent-lit office cubicles, a café, a hospital room, and once on a park bench. Technically, the most constricting situations were the cubicles, which allowed little wiggle room for lighting and shooting angles. I tried to keep my equipment to a minimum: a twenty-five-year-old Hasselblad, two lenses, a monolight, and a reflector.

The interview usually took place first, averaging an hour or more. I used a tape recorder and transcribed every word. Hoping that the subject would be more relaxed after the interview, more often than not I did the photography afterwards. But a few of the best portraits were taken before the interview.

All the volunteers received copies of the photographs. My preference was to hand-deliver them when possible because I was interested in their response. In a few cases, I returned to photograph again. Always at a reshoot, the photographer and the subject are changed by the first experience; the results are always different.

Whenever interviewees asked to approve the edited interview before publication, I complied and showed them the rough edit. Sometimes I submitted the interview for the subject's approval even though the person hadn't asked to see it. I did this for my own reassurance, to make sure that I got it right, that I was not making public something that the subject would later regret, that I had not embarrassed the interviewee. Interestingly, the changes made by interviewees mostly turned out to be grammatical. Rarely did any content get deleted or altered.

My worry about accurately and fairly representing people is a long-standing concern. A subject is always vulnerable to the camera and tape recorder, or rather to the person behind them. How words and pictures are edited very much determines how we as readers feel about the person on the page. In consecutive frames of film one can look either loving or mean-spirited depending on the split second when the photograph was taken. Or perhaps the quality of the light will influence how the reader feels about the person. I hope that these portraits fairly and respectfully give a sense of each individual. I strive not to abuse the power inherent in photographing and interviewing people.

Who are the people who appear in this book? Except for two youths who wanted to remain anonymous, they are people who were willing to be open about their HIV status and about their sexuality. Many of the participants wanted to share what they had learned from their illness. A few volunteered because they had a particular message to get out, like the person whose partner died without leaving a will and who wanted to make sure others didn't end up in the same predicament. And then there are those individuals who for whatever reasons enjoy being in the public eye.

It is not easy to be interviewed about personal matters, nor is it a simple thing to be photographed when one doesn't feel well. It takes a certain amount of energy and strength to hold forth in front of a tape recorder and camera. Therefore, the painfully shy, the extremely depressed, the frail, and the dying are not found within these pages (although several people did die between my meeting them and publication). Others who are absent are those who did not speak English, as well as those whose ethnic or religious background did not allow for public discussion of personal matters.

Before taking my first few AIDS photographs early in 1997, I braced myself for confronting illness, disfigurement, and death. In San Francisco, where I live, AIDS-related death notices appeared daily in the newspapers. In photographs I had seen of people with AIDS—by Nicholas Nixon and others—the infected often looked like concentration camp victims. One exception was Carolyn Jones's book *Living Proof* (Abbeville Press, 1994), which featured many life-affirming New Yorkers living with AIDS.

At that time in San Francisco the epidemic was most noticeable in the gay white male population. In fact, one of my first interviewees was outraged when he heard I was going to include heterosexuals. "How can you do that? AIDS is *our* disease!" he exclaimed. We quickly found out that all parts of the population were being infected—heterosexuals, women, people of color—at alarming rates. AIDS was not just a gay white disease.

The timing of my project brought another surprise. The first protease inhibitor drugs had recently become available. This meant that instead of meeting with patients near death's door, I often found myself talking with people who were, albeit tentatively, trying to imagine living, attempting to rebuild their lives. Although doctors didn't then and still don't understand the long-term effects of the new drugs, for the first time some could hope for an alternative to certain and rapid death. Although a number of the people with AIDS whom I met looked healthy because of taking protease inhibitors, I was warned early on by a writer not to be deceived by appearances. "Make sure you show their struggles," he advised.

Four years after my initial interviews, an unexpected bonus for me was having the chance to revisit a few of the individuals I had met earlier. No longer contemplating the end of their lives, they were fully engaged in living. Their struggles persisted, but they had taken new turns. The people I revisited were pondering big questions such as whether to go back to work, or whether or not to have a child. The changes in their lives were dramatic.

Not everybody was so lucky. Sadly, a number of the people in this book have died. Not everyone was a candidate for the new drugs. Many were too ill by the time they became available. Others could not tolerate them or were not helped by them.

I am grateful to those who allowed me to chronicle their lives. Just like the four youths I first heard speak at my children's high school, the forty people in this book are brave souls. They have learned to understand the nuances of living with HIV/AIDS. They have wrestled with the complicated psychological and physical manifestations of their disease, including the side effects of their many medications. They have developed new vocabularies and voices in order to speak about their lives. They have forged new relationships to help them cope. Each in his or her individual way is heroic.

The men and women in this book are leaving a legacy. I hope their words and pictures will broaden your understanding of their disease and foster compassion for those living with HIV/AIDS. Perhaps the world will become a little smarter and a little safer because of their generosity in sharing their stories.

ROSLYN BANISH
San Francisco

Witnessing an Epidemic

WE UNDERSTAND the pain of an individual, but the pain of thousands becomes little more than a statistic. While each HIV-infected person has a story to tell of grace and strength, as well as fear and anguish, these stories are too easily forgotten as individuals combine to form an epidemic. The pain of thousands is unimaginable. The horror is buried in the numbers, which have no place for the tears, hopes, worries, and loss of those touched, one by one.

In the past twenty years, HIV has killed millions worldwide and tens of thousands in San Francisco alone. To the doctor or epidemiologist, the people directly afflicted by the epidemic become "cases." And one case in such an ocean of devastation warrants only brief consideration and is seldom remembered. Yet, of course, all of these "cases" are individual people—born and loved, who themselves have loved, aspired, and worked, in the world in which we all live.

I recall, vividly, my first AIDS case. I met him on my very first day as a faculty member at San Francisco General Hospital, July 1, 1981. He was twenty-two, wasted, disfigured, and in pain from a disease none had seen before. In the three months he lived, he taught me much. He was gay and estranged from his family. He had survived by prostituting himself and had contracted every conceivable sexually transmitted disease. Yet he had strength and was as much a pioneer as any in this new medical territory. He was also sick and completely alone. As we tried to provide for his needs both in and out of the hospital, we met the gay community and the organizations that would play such a pivotal role in responding to the epidemic. We formed partnerships between the medical system and community-based groups that allowed humane care even in the absence of traditional "families."

As important as these cooperative efforts were in making the best of the situation, it was still a very bad one. In those early years, no one knew exactly what the disease was, or anything about its transmission or process. We were able only to help our patients die as comfortably as possible, in the loving presence of others. My first AIDS patient died emaciated, disfigured by Kaposi's sarcoma, suffering from pneumonia, and without even the minor comfort of knowing what was killing him.

HIV is a small virus, almost unbelievably intricate in design and damaging beyond description. Because the virus is so small it can contaminate every body fluid, including the blood and the male and female genital fluids. HIV is not controlled or cured like most infections. Rather it continues to reproduce, or replicate, even after the body's immune system attempts to respond.

HIV infection is, at first, almost silent—few people even remember when they were first invaded. And this silence has tragic consequences. Its victims—and only in this sense is the word appropriate—are unknowingly infected and able to spread the infection, again unknowingly, to others. Thus the stage is set for an epidemic more devastating than any in human history. The gradual, inconspicuous nature of the HIV disease process after infection is the final necessary condition to the pandemic. Unlike diseases such as Ebola virus, which kill horribly and quickly, HIV kills slowly (and ultimately as horribly), allowing the successful passage of the virus to many others without generating the immediate social reaction caused by sensational rapid killers.

To the doctor, a person becomes a patient following a diagnosis. To the person, however, the diagnosis is only one event in the context of an entire life. We miss much if that context is ignored. People who carry the HIV virus come from all walks of life and have experiences before infection as unique and varied as fingerprints. In many instances, they have honed their survival skills. Too often, as a result of their illness, they have experienced abuse, abandonment, hatred, and stigma. Yet in most cases they hold to life with ferocious tenacity. They are true survivors and have much to teach.

When people are confronted by disaster, amazing transformations can occur. We all know stories of heroes who have emerged in the face of catastrophe. The HIV epidemic has also spawned unlikely heroes. Even those struggling with addiction or other serious problems have discovered new strength when presented with the apparent death sentence of HIV. Given the opportunity, most reject a quiet death. And in looking back at their prior lives, many gain a new perspective on themselves and their circumstances. Lost in the vast numbers of the epidemic is the reality that HIV has created heroes one by one.

Another of my early patients had lived with his AIDS for several years. His Kaposi's sarcoma had stabilized with only minimal therapy, and he had continued to work at a small business he owned. Then, on one of his visits to my office, I was shocked to find he had suffered a rapid, explosive spread of his tumor. He had new, cancerous-appearing skin lesions covering much of his face, chest, and back. He also was short of breath simply talking to me—sure evidence in those days of pneumocystis pneumonia. There was little doubt on his part or mine what had happened. Nine of his closest friends had died of AIDS in one week, and he had lost hope. His humor, grace, and quiet heroism were still in evidence, but his fight was quickly over as he joined his friends in death.

Viewed from afar, the HIV epidemic is sometimes described as a grand battle. Militaristic terms are evoked—the attack, the casualty counts, the counteroffensives. But it is only when the epidemic is viewed at close range—in the homes, families, and workplaces of the HIV-infected—that we begin to see the full human dimension of what has befallen us. In this, we can see a parallel with the tragedy of September 11, 2001. For many months after the terrorist attacks, the *New York Times* published short, poignant remembrances of individual victims together with small photos, which were later collected in a book. In San Francisco in the 1980s, in response to the HIV epidemic, the *Bay Area Reporter*, a gay community newspaper, began publishing AIDS obituaries. By the early 1990s, these AIDS memorials typically filled two entire pages of the paper.

The devastation in San Francisco reverberated also through businesses, professional organizations, and churches. One Lutheran congregation lost 10 percent of its members annually and employed a full-time pastor to minister to those who were dying. The depths of the epidemic were indeed dark. Medical treatment merely slowed the progression of the disease: one had to expect that each new patient would progressively sicken and certainly die.

Then came 1996. In January of that year, initial reports of success with a new class of HIV drugs were met with near disbelief in the medical community. We had seen "advances" before. Yet with the presentation of even more compelling data only six months later at a landmark conference in Vancouver, British Columbia, we were able to begin to believe. Seemingly overnight, the epidemic was transformed. The inevitable sentence of horrifying decline and ultimate death had been replaced by a kind of reprieve: possibly chronic disease. Doctors and medical researchers, in private conversations, even began to speak hopefully of a cure. Veterans in the AIDS battle were breathless with excitement.

Many of our patients, fortunate in surviving to this incredible moment, quickly passed from planning to die to deciding how to live. Going *off* disability, retraining in more interesting careers, and thinking about a future became the new focus of energy. As with any major transition, this shift was not without its own stress. Patients soon discovered that a regimen of taking several drugs each day religiously on time—drugs that had their own side effects—was far from the "normal" life enjoyed by others. But no one would want to go back in time to the early epidemic before the introduction of protease inhibitors.

Today, our optimism, while still strong, is more tempered. HIV is—or at least can be—now a chronic disease. When diagnosed sufficiently early and when treated appropriately, in a patient sufficiently motivated to take treatment exactly as prescribed, HIV can be controlled. The immune system can recover, and the risks of death can be dramatically forestalled. But all this all presupposes that the infected person has access to experienced providers and the drugs, tests, and other elements of care.

The larger problem, of course, is that only a small fraction of the world's HIV-infected population will ever benefit from the advances we have realized. Worldwide, more than 90 percent of those infected are unaware of their infection, and most live in areas without access to safe drinking water or a stable food supply, much less "triple therapy" for AIDS. Even in the United States, the most advantaged country, thousands live on our streets with untreated HIV disease, coming to hospitals only in the final stages of AIDS. For HIV-infected people in Africa, Asia, and parts of Europe, the absence of realistic hope for full access to our breakthrough interventions is a constant cruel reminder of their fate. Women, unable to insist on simple barrier protection, are infected by their husbands and give birth to infected children, because they lack access to a simple pill that could easily prevent this spread. And, infected or not, countless children are growing up as orphans, rejected by others for the "sins" of their mothers who have died in the epidemic.

How will this end? Not by our wishes alone, fervent as they may be. We saw thousands of our patients die earlier in the epidemic, despite their hopes, despite ours. And we already know that such losses will be repeated 40 million times in the world, even were HIV transmission to end today and even if a completely protective vaccine were in our hands—which is not and will not be the case for years, if ever.

So, what can we do? We can work even harder to find a cure. We can raise funds to extend our treatments more broadly. We can help to educate others in HIV prevention. We can and should do all this and more. But we must begin and end with the person. We must focus on each individual struggling with HIV. We must know them as the individuals they are. We must pay attention to the stories that are their experience. Only with this grounding can our efforts succeed.

I invite you to listen to the voices of the people who have consented to be included in this book. With them, and others like them, we can move toward the light we hope to see at the end of the epidemic.

PAUL A. VOLBERDING, M.D.
San Francisco
AUGUST 2002

PORTRAITS

& INTERVIEWS

MAURICE ANTHONY

Maurice Anthony

I'M TWENTY-ONE YEARS OLD and I'm from St. Louis, Missouri. I am the oldest of nine kids. Me and my father, we don't keep in contact with each other because he doesn't want to be involved with me because, number one I'm gay and number two, because I'm HIV positive. My mother turned to alcohol and drugs. I got taken away from her when I was five because of the alcoholism and because she physically abused us. I was raised by foster parents and in children's homes. So I was a "behavior disorder child." Basically that is a child that always was bad, always did things to get folks' attention.

It all started for me when I turned sixteen. That is when I got my HIV diagnosis. During that time I was staying with my uncle. When he did find out, he couldn't deal with it. He was afraid that I might infect his newborn child as well as his other kids. The executive director of the organization I now work for, Blacks Assisting Blacks Against AIDS, got me hooked up with different services in the St. Louis metropolitan area, and then I got my own place through Doorways, which gets money from the Ryan White funds. So basically I have been on my own for five years.

You have to be HIV positive to stay in one of these apartments. Once I come back to my place, I'm reminded that I'm HIV positive. So it's a home in the sense that this is what I have, but it's hard, you know, coming from somewhere where I'm having a good time and then walking through those doors and realizing that, hey, I'm HIV positive.

When my mother found out I was HIV positive, she instantly started crying. It was hard because she would never talk about it. Now everything is different. She accepts my gay friends, she accepts who I am. She always asks me how I'm doing. She wants me to take good care of myself. And she's supportive with everything I do. A dramatic change. But she's still drinking. I think she drinks heavier now than she ever did because of my diagnosis. She knows that there is a possibility that the son she wished was dead, could be dead.

BEFORE I FOUND OUT ABOUT MY HIV, I WAS JUST ANOTHER YOUTH. I WAS AN ANGRY YOUTH. I WAS ABUSED SEXUALLY, MENTALLY, EMOTIONALLY, PHYSICALLY. I HATED MY FAMILY. I CAN HONESTLY SAY THAT THIS DISEASE HAS GIVEN ME A NEW OUTLOOK ON LIFE.

Being gay is not what you want to be because you're not accepted, you're looked at as a punk or sissy, as my father states, not a man. It's not an "in" thing to be gay. My gay friends are my family. They may say some painful things sometimes, but I know they'll be there. I have this feeling that when I die, my mother will be drunk and she just won't be there. She's told me on many occasions that she just can't take it. Emotions—she just can't take it.

When I found out my HIV diagnosis, I was a junior in high school. I had nobody to talk to. I felt I was on my last breath. Oh God, what am I going to do? So I confided in the junior counselor at my school. I remember her sharing her story with me about somebody in her family being HIV positive. I felt like, hey, she can trust me so I can trust her. So I told her that I was HIV positive. When I came back to school the next Monday there was a rumor going around that somebody in the school was HIV positive. The counselor had told a teacher that I was HIV positive. So a student came in first-hour class and said, "Hey dude, Miss Such-and-Such said you were HIV positive."

By this time I'm hysterical, I'm hurting. I felt everybody was looking at me, everybody was afraid to talk to me, touch me. I felt like I was given a death sentence right then and there. I most definitely couldn't stay at that school. So I left and never went back to another school. I have a lot of anger because I would have been one of the first people in my mother's family to graduate high school. I'm sure you can see the anger through my facial expressions. I want to find me a lawyer so I can sue the school district because that shouldn't have happened. I don't want money but I want justice.

Now here I am today. I am still struggling, but I have more strength than I ever thought I could have in this world. My T cell count is higher, 564. My weight stands firm, 185. I feel healthy, I feel "gorgeous," like I tell everybody else.

I would like to do some modeling. I do poetry. I've written over 350 poems already. Actually I do enjoy writing when I have feelings. I also love music. It's another way I express how I feel. I love R and B, a particular artist Toni Braxton but mainly Regina Belle. She tells it all.

I've had a lot of suicidal tendencies. Like when I first found out about my disease, I wanted to kill myself. But I'm too strong for that. I have a lot to look forward to, and killing myself wouldn't solve anything.

God is the reason why I'm here so far. I believe He has chosen me to do the work I do. I believe there's a heaven and a hell and I believe I will be going to heaven.

Before I found out about my HIV, I was just another youth. I was an angry youth. I was abused sexually, mentally, emotionally, physically. I hated my family. I can honestly say that this disease has given me a new outlook on life. Now when I tell people that, they say, "Are you happy you are HIV positive?" No, I'm not happy that I'm HIV positive, but I can truly say that it has given me a lot of positive thoughts on what life is and how important it is.

I think God does things to us to open our eyes. I never question Him. Oh yeah, when I first found out I questioned Him everyday. He might have very well saved my life from death. I don't know. But I'm grateful for whatever it is and that's the truth.

POEM BY MAURICE ANTHONY

But, I Know Eventually I'll Die

Look into my eyes,
And, tell me what you see,
It's me facing this deadly disease,

I have nowhere to run,
Or nowhere to hide,
It's mostly me and my tough pride,

I'm young and gay,
But, I'm living my life by the day,
So, it's hard to say,
Where I'll lay,

I don't know what to expect,
Or even what to think,
But one thing's for sure, I don't need a
shrink,

So it's hard to get by,
Even on a little lie,
But, still I try,

While I cry, and cry, and cry,
But, I know eventually I'll die.

Cleve Jones

[FOUNDER OF THE NAMES PROJECT AIDS MEMORIAL QUILT]

I LIVE IN A SMALL VILLAGE in Sonoma County, a few miles from where the Russian River meets the Pacific on the California coast. It's about one hundred households, and I spend a lot of time with my neighbors. There are many people with HIV that live on the Russian River. And these are the people I see every day when I'm at home. It's a very diverse little family ranging in age from seven to fifty-five. We do kayaking on the river together, we have big dinners and celebrate many of the holidays together. We support each other during times of crisis.

I live in an old house on the river, and I have giant redwood trees in my backyard. Right now my time is really divided between downtime, when I'm not feeling really great, and uptime. When I'm not feeling great I tend to stay home and futz around in the garden and hide a bit.

When I'm feeling well I go out on the road with quilt displays for presentations to colleges and high schools. The talk I give is basically the story of starting the quilt. It touches on a number of the political and social issues that have accompanied the epidemic. And then I usually spend another hour with the students taking questions. And they always have a lot of questions. They're always amazingly informed and supportive and compassionate.

I just got back from a trip to Utah, visiting high schools there. I fully expected it to be a very difficult trip. I had made a pledge to this fourteen-year-old girl named Veronica Hernandez I met in Washington. We met in the lobby of the hotel where all of the NAMES Project volunteers were staying. I started talking to her. She said she had come to bring her mother's quilt and told me her mother and father had both been killed by HIV. She lived in Ogden, Utah, and wanted to know if it was possible to bring her mother's quilt back to Utah to show in her high school. I said if she were able to get permission from the principal that I would come with the quilt, that I would want to see her, and that I thought she was very brave. And I got a letter from the principal of her school inviting me to come to Ogden and talk to all of the students.

Almost everyone I met in Utah was a heterosexual, believing Mormon and kind and respectful and so anxious for the young people in their charge to hear my story. They had up on the marquee of the Ogden High School "Welcome Cleve Jones, Founder of the AIDS Memorial Quilt."

It was a required assembly. None of them knew Veronica's story. It was a real eye-opener for these kids because Veronica is a lovely, bright, and very popular girl in the school. When their coach announced to the assembled students that the quilt was for the mother of a student there, you could hear a pin drop. And when he said her name, there was a gasp. She came out and explained her story.

I had the idea for the quilt on November 27, 1985, at the Candlelight March for Harvey Milk and George Moscone, San Francisco's supervisor and mayor who were assassinated. I made the first quilt in honor of my best friend, Marvin Feldman, who

CLEVE JONES

had died. And it was first displayed on October 11, 1987, which was my thirty-third birthday.

Yeah, yeah, yeah. I knew it would be a big project. From the beginning I clearly believed that tens of thousands of people would participate and tens of thousands of quilt panels would be created. But, after saying that, I was also completely clueless as to what that meant. I knew back then that millions were going to die, and I knew that the quilt would be a good vehicle for all of us who were suffering so much. But I

didn't know what that bigness would mean in terms of lives of people and the extraordinary number of people I have been connected to through the quilt and the incredible effort that goes into it. I mean, it's one thing to have this idea that you are going to put a blanket on the National Mall, but when you figure out how many volunteers it takes and how many trucks and how many hours of volunteer labor, it's quite amazing.

I knew if gay people were involved that it would be visually stunning, of course, but I had no idea of the artistry that would go into it. Nothing prepared me for that. Back in the '80s when I started it I was really focused on "evidence," because I was in the Castro and everyone was dead or dying. People were just dying every day. And they just didn't care about it in the press. The *Times* didn't write about it. It wasn't really until Rock Hudson died that the media had a little bit of attention. We needed evidence, something we could take to the Capitol and say, "This is the consequence of your inaction. Look at the suffering and loss that is represented in this quilt. And also see in it the love and determination and courage of those of us who are continuing to fight." I didn't really predict the spiritual power that it has assumed over the years.

Now it's so horrendously difficult to display the quilt in its entirety that we've pretty much put any thoughts of doing that again on hold for now. But we do smaller- scale displays somewhere in this country every week—synagogues, churches, high school gymnasiums, colleges, small towns, big towns. We do more targeted displays focusing around, for example, African Americans or Jewish people or Latino people. And we have the quilt digitalized so people can access it on the Internet.

Unlike the other eighteen thousand AIDS organizations in the United States, we possess fifty tons of fabric that has been sewn together by real people who have a real expressed concern about what happens to the quilt. So I think our position at this point is that we are going to continue accepting quilts and using them as part of our educational campaigns for the duration of the epidemic. The fact that there are fewer quilts coming in is a very happy thing. The death rate from AIDS continues to go down. I'm grateful and amazed that I've lived long enough to even have to contemplate what we do with the quilt when it's over. We have the world's largest community arts project that's entrusted to us. We have to preserve it.

I'm not really a public health educator. I'm just a person who had a good idea and was fortunate enough to find people who shared it and made it work. But I think one message that the kids get from me is, "I have some information for you about HIV and AIDS and gay people." But I think another important message is, "If you ever get a good idea, stick to it, even though everybody else tells you it's a stupid idea."

In the beginning nobody liked the idea of the quilt. They thought it was morbid. I had been an activist for over a decade in San Francisco before the epidemic. I had a large network of talented and wonderful friends and activists. I was always calling them as I was always being called upon by them to do these projects over the years. The people who finally emerged to take on the project did not include a single person from my past. They were all brand new people who came out of nowhere to make this thing happen. They had been touched by the epidemic.

I guess when I was first told I had AIDS back in '85, I then immediately assumed that I would die very quickly and sort of lived like that for a really long time. Just waiting, checking every square inch of my body every morning in the shower, looking in my mouth with a flashlight for thrush and other infections. People died a lot faster then, so this wasn't just paranoia. You'd see somebody in January and they looked fine. In February they didn't look so good, and by March they'd be gone. So I just sort of kept waiting for it. All you could do was fight, you know, try to do the work that had to be done—organizing and protesting, trying to find doctors for people and housing. So from '84 to '92 I was just waiting for the other shoe to drop. Nothing dramatic went wrong, but I knew that I was declining. And then I got really sick and turned forty around the same time. It felt like I went from being very young to very old in about a week.

And now I think of myself as an older person. It's hard not having any friends left from when I was twenty. If there's no one left in your life who knew you when you were young, that part of you sort of doesn't exist anymore. You can't corroborate your memory, you can't laugh about "remember when." Now, of course, my mother and father are still alive and my sister. But they weren't my peers.

I ran for supervisor here in San Francisco in 1992. The campaign really exhausted me. I went into it with 600 T cells and had only 300 when it was over. I just narrowly lost. Then I got very, very sick. I was allergic to almost all the treatments. I tried to garden, and I kept passing out and waking up with my face mashed into the begonias. Not good for the begonias.

Right now I feel good about 75 percent of the time. I'm having a rough time right now because I started a new treatment combination and it's been a little difficult. But it's very promising. Everybody just has to stay alive until the drugs get more effective and less toxic. I have been very hopeful and active again and am having my ambition return in terms of wanting to succeed in delivering on a few things here before my time is up.

Even before I hitchhiked out of Phoenix at age seventeen, I've been an activist. I started out as a kid with my parents working for civil rights, against the war. So, it was just like, "This is so fucked up I can't believe it." The only thing I know how to do is draft petitions, organize volunteers, hold marches, get the bullhorns. Whether it's a virus named HIV or a virus named Anita Bryant, my response is the same. My mother and father have in their lives shown great determination and willingness to fight against all odds and persevere against popular opinion if necessary or doctor's advice or whatever. They're both very strong people. It's a great blessing going through this knowing that your family is completely and totally 100 percent on your team. I don't think either one of them has ever been particularly comfortable with marching in the street. They don't like crowds. But they go to AIDS marches now.

When I come back to the city, I go to Castro Street. It's amazing how many people I know that I will run into. And I think living in the country, while it's been very good for me in many ways, has contributed a little bit to feeling isolated. I have close friends and support there now, but I have twenty-five years of history in San Francisco. So when I come back I get really exhilarated just from seeing all these people. I go to Louie's Barber Shop and get a haircut and just see how many people stop to say "hi." And it's really nice. Or I go to Cafe Flore and have a latte and run into a former boyfriend or two. And that's really nice. And then I'll think this great city is so beautiful. They didn't all die. There's still people that remember me. There's still people to hang out with and have fun with.

I am so privileged. Hardly a day goes by when I'm just not amazed by the gratitude people have to me for the quilt. You know, I still don't know how to sew. I had the idea but I did precious little of the work. Anyone who has ever worked at the NAMES Project can confirm for you, I get to fly around and take credit for the whole damn thing. Had I died once it was launched, it would have gone forward without me. The other day I was washing dishes in the window. I saw three little kids, eight or nine years

IS THERE A FAMILY LEFT IN THIS COUNTRY THAT DOESN'T KNOW SOMEONE WITH AIDS? PEOPLE HAVE COME OUT ABOUT THEIR HIV STATUS AND IT'S VERY MUCH LIKE THE GAY STRUGGLE IN THAT WE WIN WHEN WE ARE OPEN AND HONEST ABOUT OUR LIVES.

old, and one said, "Hey, do you know who lives there?" "That's the guy who started the AIDS quilt. He's famous. He knows the president."

Oh, it feels great. But it's not always pleasant. I meet people sometimes and I tell them who I am and they burst into tears. It's just unlikely that I'm ever going to meet anybody again without, within the first fifteen minutes, hearing about friends they lost, or their lover who died before the drugs were available, or their own problems tolerating the drugs. People want to talk to me about their losses. I'm required to listen, to try very hard to listen.

I like being around young people because gay men my age, when we get together, although there is still hope in our hearts now, all we talk about is medications, who has got lymphoma this month. The young people talk about the future.

In our group I think most of us are patient, pissed off, hopeful, scared. There's not a lot of time to be unproductively emotional. In our group of, say, twelve people, there's really only two of us that are activist types. We're just trying to stay alive and do the work that needs to be done. We are preoccupied with things like making sure that a seven-year-old friend of ours with HIV is allowed to go to school and not be abused by the other children. We believe he's going to have a normal life. We're trying to get Glaxo Wellcome to make available their latest drug so our friend Larry, who lives a mile upstream, who has failed every single drug that has been made available, will have one more chance. It's issues like getting money for housing for friends from HUD, getting people signed up for benefits, figuring out how to pay for medication. It's very time consuming and requires one to stay pretty focused. Anger is always there, but I think people realize how much they have to focus on the work of staying alive and moving this forward.

People need to step back and look at what has come out of this. As a homosexual looking at it, what I see is that a small, despised, ostracized minority attained freedom in the process of fighting a disease that killed too many of us. When this whole thing first started, I remember conversations. "Oh, no one will move to the Castro anymore." Or, "The gay neighborhoods will cease to exist. Nobody will want to associate with us. We're going to lose the little political power we've got." None of that happened. Instead people came out of the closet, took up the banners, fought till they died, passed the banner on to the next, and moved forward.

Is there a family left in this country that doesn't know someone with AIDS? People have come out about their HIV status and it's very much like the gay struggle in that we win when we are open and honest about our lives. When heterosexuals come to know gay and lesbian people, they cease fearing us. The people that I think have made the difference have been ordinary people with AIDS who are so courageous about revealing their status to their world. By doing so they compelled and required this country and our society to move forward.

I'm very aware that gay people are just a fraction of what's happening in the AIDS world. We have quilt initiatives in forty-four countries now. I met a woman from a Central African country last year who said, "If a cure for AIDS was as simple as a glass of clean water, it would not be available in my country." So globally the picture is much more grim.

My future? I'd like to think of a way to make a living now that HIV is going to be defeated and I'm going to have to get a real job, as my father chuckled at me the other day. I'm forty-two. I don't have any money. I'd like to make enough money so that I can take care of my parents when they retire and need assistance. And who knows, if there was a cure, and if I were able to make some money, I might just try to go back into politics. God, somebody shoot me!

NICHOLAS METCALF

Nicholas Metcalf

I'M FROM ROSEBUD, South Dakota. I am an enrolled member of the Sicangu Oyate "Burnt Thigh." I grew up on a reservation. I have fourteen brothers and sisters. My family for the most part is still on the reservation and I go home a couple of times a year to visit them.

One of my sisters works at the school as a teacher's aide and another works with housing. My older brother is going to school now to become a radiologist. My brother and I are the only ones who left the reservation, but my sisters have tried. Life off the rez is so different. What I miss most about the rez is being around my family.

I stayed on the reservation until I went to college. Yes, it was a big deal to leave. But I wanted to find other people like me. I knew there had to be other people like me somewhere. So I went to college and came out of the closet as gay the first year I was there. Within the first month of college I met my first partner and I was with him for three years. He was instrumental in helping me with my transition from the reservation. I started doing HIV and queer stuff and organizing right away.

If I hadn't left the reservation, I think my life would be very different. I would probably be working with the tribe somewhere, looking like a sissy and drinking way too much and looking about forty years old. My mother's friends when I was growing up were these really effeminate, flamboyant native men. Everybody knew they were gay, but we never really talked about it. They got lots of teasing.

After college in South Dakota, I ended up in the "big city" [Minneapolis]. I was only going for a year, but that was seven years ago and I'm still here. This summer I got my master's degree in social work. That was a great accomplishment considering all that has been going on in my life.

I'm twenty-nine years old and I have known I'm HIV positive for about three years. At the time of my diagnosis I was assistant director to a local HIV/AIDS service organization. Once I learned of my status, I was in shock the first few weeks and then had my first big breakdown, one of three breakdowns. I didn't even have the language to talk about what it felt like. I was infected by my ex-partner. I knew he was positive when I went into the relationship. It's not like I didn't know. Me and my ex-partner looked into having children, but then in the end he didn't want children and I did.

Now I'm a dad of a two-year-old. I adopted my nephew when he was born. I took him home from the hospital. It was a decision that I feel proud of and I love being a dad. My son has taught me what love is and how beautiful life is.

What kind of parent do I try to be? Loving and affirming with the hope of creating vibrant children who love themselves, community, and spirit! Imparting Native American culture is very core to that. My father was a tribal councilman and community health representative. My mother works with housing on the reservation. So growing up in that family, community was important. You draw a sense of identity from the community. You work for the people, your life is about the people, so that your people will survive. To sustain a community you have to work collaboratively. This is a lesson that was instilled in me when I was a child and I continue to live by.

Being a parent, I think about safety issues, not only for myself personally but also for my child. Living with HIV and caring for my son, I find myself being extremely cautious. If I cut myself in a household accident, is my kid safe? Another concern is that having enough energy to be a good parent can be an issue. I feel OK right now, but I'm at a point where I have to get new medication.

IF I HADN'T LEFT THE RESERVATION, I THINK MY LIFE WOULD BE VERY DIFFERENT. I WOULD PROBABLY BE WORKING WITH THE TRIBE SOMEWHERE, LOOKING LIKE A SISSY AND DRINKING WAY TOO MUCH AND LOOKING ABOUT FORTY YEARS OLD.

My typical day usually starts at 6. My son gets up at 6:30. We play around for a little while and then we have breakfast. I do dishes and then I start getting him ready for the day, for day care. Then I get myself showered and ready. This huge process takes an hour. And then I go to work. Stay till about 5:30. Pick up Sunny, make dinner, we play a little bit and start getting ready for bed at 8:30. He's in bed by 9. Then I get my hour to relax and do whatever I need to do. Those days of sleeping in are gone. But I think about my life now as a twenty-nine-year-old compared to my mother's; she had eight children by the time she was twenty-nine.

Besides being a single dad, I work full-time as executive director of Minnesota Men of Color. We work with queer people of color. We help them find a space where they can be safe. We are funded to do HIV/STD prevention education and health education for people living with HIV/AIDS. We receive state and county funding. Specifically we work with African American, Chicano/Latino, and Native American men and women. We're also trying to make connections to the Asian American community. We work with all communities of color, trying to create safe spaces for them, create leadership, and provide services. The HIV part of the services is a big part of it.

We're a small shop. There are only four of us here. Obviously we're limited in what we can do. The nice part is that we, the staff, have the luxury to work in an affirming place, to be out about our sexuality and our status.

Being a man of color can be very isolating. One of the things about isolation is not having others to talk about what you're experiencing. But we're slowly building communities. The question is, with limited resources, how can we sustain them? Lots of work to do. But it feels like there is progress.

There's not that one huge community of color, so it's important that we build bridges and support each other's communities. For example, next weekend a Black Gay Pride brunch is being hosted by the Two Spirit Community. My big thing is about building cooperation *between* communities.

Diversity is also found within the Native American community, where there are over five hundred federally recognized tribes and many more who have lost this status and are working at getting it back. With all these different tribes, the politics of getting our issues and needs met has to be done collaboratively—at least I hope. No, I am not trying to bring everybody together. Organizing queer people of color is already big enough.

My family is very affirming of my life and they're very proud of me. I know a couple of years ago when me and my partner were talking about getting married, I wanted to have a ceremony on the reservation. My mother was happy. She was looking forward to having this big wedding. But my parents aren't typical. I oftentimes thank the Creator for having been born into such a wonderful family. Sure we have problems and we struggle like everyone else, but my mother binds us together and reminds us of our commonality.

I'm much more deliberate about my life now. I have different choices to make, but you make it up as you go along. Like today I am dealing with child care. OK, do I put my son in home day care or institutional day care?

Kim Olivares

I JUST TURNED FORTY in January. When I was twenty-five, I went back to school at night to do a paralegal program. Now I work for a law firm. For many years I thought about going to law school. I also thought about being a police officer, but I saw what it did to my father. He developed ulcers and became an alcoholic. And I really didn't want people shooting at me. I thought about juvenile probation because I really enjoy kids, but I didn't know if I could handle that emotionally so I ended up where I'm at.

My father passed away about five months before I found out I was positive. That was a little more than three years ago. Actually, I'd really like to have him around now. I was his only daughter, the baby in the family, and whether or not he'd ever admit it, I think I was his favorite. But I think knowing I had HIV would have killed him. And because he despised my ex-husband, the person who infected me,

I think he would have probably blown his brains out. So maybe it's better he is not here.

About six months before I found out I was positive, as a benefit of my employment we were given long-term disability, which was a very, very good policy. This has made all the difference. I make good money. I am able to own my own home. I have good medical insurance. And I am blessed with good health that I hope continues.

When I went back to work that first day after my diagnosis, I just sat all the partners down and said, "This is what is going on." And my boss just sat there and cried. And throughout the day, I remember going into his office to put something on our calendar, and I meant to write "mediation" and I put "arbitration," and I said, "I'll stop making these stupid mistakes, I promise." And he looked at me and said, "Don't worry about it." And he started crying again.

I consider myself to be extremely lucky. With the exception of one individual, I have not had to face on a personal level any kind of prejudice or bigotry. I have a big support group: my mother and my older brother, Michael, my twenty-three-year-old stepson, Joel—I have permanent guardianship of him—and my friends. Initially for my stepson it was extremely difficult because his biological mother had died from cancer when he was nine. So now he thought he was going to lose his second mother. He was very, very upset and very frightened. He would come in, shower, change, and leave, and I finally yanked him in one day and said, "OK. Let's talk about this because you are avoiding me." And we talked it out.

My mother had a very hard time with my diagnosis because we were still going through that grieving process with my father's death. But she's an incredibly strong woman and always has been and I think she sees this as another battle to be fought. She never lets me see her be upset. To put this in perspective, I am forty years old and I have seen my mother cry three times in my life. So even if she is crying, she's not letting me see it.

KIM OLIVARES

The first week or so she would not leave. I would walk around the house. I would have my dog behind me, my mother behind the dog. I started joking with her that if I stopped short, I was going to have the dog and her stuck in my ass. But she needed to be there. She wanted to go to all of my doctor appointments. She had me taking so many vitamins I thought I was being punished at a certain point. Finally I sat down with her one day and said, "Mom, this is my disease. I have to be in control of the situation." She said, "OK. When I'm bothering you, tell me to back off."

And so now I go to my doctor appointments alone. But I call her and let her know what's happening. She's become very active in a local AIDS organization; she answers phones, stuffs envelopes. My father used to call her Florence Nightingale. She is very up on her medical knowledge, very up on nutrition.

WHEN I GO INTO THE PUBLIC SCHOOLS I NOT ONLY TALK ABOUT WHAT IT IS LIKE TO LIVE WITH HIV BUT OUR OBLIGATION TO HIV POSITIVE INDIVIDUALS TO BE LESS JUDGMENTAL AND MORE COMPASSIONATE. IN THESE CLASSES I SAY, "LOOK AT ME. I AM THIS WHITE, MIDDLE-AGED, MIDDLE-CLASS WOMAN WHO WAS MARRIED. I THOUGHT I WAS SAFE. SO IF YOU THINK FOR A MINUTE IT CAN'T HAPPEN TO YOU, YOU HAD BETTER THINK AGAIN."

When I found out I was positive, I was already divorced from my husband. So I phoned him to tell him what was going on. Then he got tested and found out he was positive. After we were first married, it became clear that he had substance abuse problems. He snorted a tremendous amount of cocaine, he drank a tremendous amount of alcohol. Lord knows what else he did when he was impaired. He also admitted that prior to us being married he used prostitutes.

My ex-husband was born in El Salvador and came to this country when he was eighteen. I was very concerned about him because I knew he didn't have anybody he could talk to and he was freaked out about being positive. I knew this bar he hung out at in South San Francisco, so I went out there one night after work, and sure enough he was there. I was really rather shocked at his appearance. He looked sick, he hadn't shaved for a couple of days, he had lost about twenty pounds. He just looked like hell.

I tried to tell him, "You can't do this. You might as well get it over with and blow your brains out and stop punishing and torturing everybody." And I have repeatedly provided him with information about where he can get free services. He won't take responsibility for it.

When I first was diagnosed, I went into panic mode. I found out in August and figured I'd be dead by December. So about a month or two later I had a very extensive estate plan put together with a trust. I also isolated myself tremendously because I figured that if people knew about me, they wouldn't be around for me. At a certain point I decided that, OK, I can deal with this, but I need to make something good come out of this. So that's when I had the idea of talking to teenagers about AIDS. I had always related well to teenagers. The psychologist I was seeing said, "I think it's a great idea. I'd like you to talk to my class at Skyline College."

So I went and told my story for the first time. And it was incredibly cathartic. I wish I had done it earlier. I wish I had been ready to do it earlier. It took such a weight off of me to finally come out and say it in public. And my stepson who was attending the same college came to that class and allowed me to identify him. A student asked him, "Wasn't it hard for you having both parents positive?" And he said, "Yes it is, but it is easier with Kim because she focuses on living and my father focuses on dying."

Another thing that HIV has made me do is realize just how precious time is. I really don't know how much time I have, and I do not know what the quality of it will be. So I have stopped putting things off. In the last few years I went to France, England, and Scotland. I want to travel more. It's also made me start thinking about doing things that I have been just petrified of doing, like skydiving.

I have also become more of an advocate. I've never been known to keep my mouth shut when I think something is wrong. In fact, my mouth has probably been my worst enemy over the years. I think this advocacy is now tempered with a certain amount of maturity. When I go into the public schools I not only talk about what it is like to live with HIV but our obligation to HIV positive individuals to be less judgmental and more compassionate.

In these classes I say, "Look at me. I am this white, middle-aged, middle-class woman who was married. I thought I was safe. So if you think for a minute it can't happen to you, you had better think again." I tell them, "This is the ultimate nondiscriminatory virus. It doesn't care what color your skin is, it doesn't care how much money your mommy makes, where you live, how old you are. The only thing it wants from you is to be alive and healthy so that it can kill you." It frightens me to think about how many young people are out there who still believe the party line that it only happens to gays and IV drug users.

I tell these teenagers, "You know, when I was your age the worst thing that could happen to me was that I could get pregnant. Then in my twenties the worst thing that could happen to me was herpes. Uncomfortable but not deadly. I hit my thirties and the worst thing that could happen to me was contracting AIDS. And it happened."

One thing that is a common lament with many positive people I know is that your sex life is over to a certain degree. Maybe for gay men it's easier because AIDS has been in their community so much longer and it's more acceptable. I personally haven't had a date or sex in a long time. While I miss sex, I don't miss it as much as I miss having the emotional intimacy with somebody that you have when you are in a good relationship.

I have a lot of concern about how a man would react to me, knowing I was HIV positive. I remember one night asking my roommate, "Well, when should I disclose this to somebody?" And she looked at me and said, "When would you want someone to disclose it to you?" And I said, "Probably the first time he kissed me." I don't know if it's because I have made bad choices in the past regarding the men I've become involved with, or I just don't have a lot of faith in men, but it scares the shit out of me to think that I would have to disclose my HIV diagnosis.

Not a day goes by that it doesn't cross my mind that I am positive. Now, in what context and how, it varies from day to day. It could be driving to work and thinking about my stepson. It starts a domino effect, and by the time I get to work I'm in tears because I may never see my grandchildren.

I would really like to put my energies into doing something that would make a difference. I would like to learn how to lobby about AIDS education and prevention. I want to get the attention of the people who are running this state and this country and tell them, "You can't keep doing this. You can't cut prevention money." It really fries my ass that I can't pass out condoms in public schools. One of the biggest reasons most kids don't buy condoms is they are embarrassed. So I say to them, "Do you really think the clerk at Longs Drug Store gives a shit whether you are buying condoms or not? She is probably thinking about her own hot date that night." When I talk to the kids, I do say abstinence is also an option.

There were members of my family and friends who did not know about my status. As time has gone by, it became more and more difficult to try to keep track of who knows and who doesn't know. I realized that I painted myself into that corner. So before I turned forty, my mother asked me what I wanted for my birthday. And I told her a really big party. So she threw this party to end all parties. At the celebration I decided to tell everybody about my HIV status. "Look, this is what is going on, this is how it is." It was wonderful. The gift I gave to myself was that I set myself free.

[FOUR YEARS LATER]

Now I look at my disease as being a chronic problem as opposed to a life-and-death situation. It's been a long road getting here.

Four years ago I had an HIV diagnosis, which became an AIDS diagnosis one year later. My T cells dropped to 196, and I was extremely angry because it was four lousy T cells that gave me the diagnosis. But I also knew that something was wrong. I was very tired. I had a significant case of thrush in my mouth. I was beginning to have chronic yeast and bladder infections. I got past so much of that only to have it slap me in the face again. And then there was also this sense of relief because I felt like I had been running from AIDS. I knew at some point there was going to be the AIDS diagnosis. I was always looking over my shoulder.

I began to take a drug cocktail. I wasn't happy about it. The worst thing I have to deal with is chronic diarrhea. But I still have a life, I still enjoy good health, I'm still very active, but I just have to watch what I expose myself to.

So many other changes in my life have affected me so much. My mother has had two strokes. Now, I've been close to my mother even though we've had our issues. She's always been a very strong, independent individual. And now at seventy-one suddenly she has become dependent. Looking after her takes a big part of my life, even though we have hired some caregivers. Sometimes I feel this obligation or guilt if I'm not with her. And it has really affected how I don't dwell on myself. There's this other big thing out there.

Another thing that changed was I just got tired of being overweight and feeling ugly and fat and unwanted. So I got off my ass and lost weight and found something that cleared up my skin. I actually started dating. But it was very hard for me to meet men, because I don't attend church, which is a place where one would meet men. And I'm certainly not going to hang out in bars. So I was at my computer one day and came across personal ads. I thought, "Hell, I can do this!" I placed this ad and I got forty responses, which I thought was great because it was based on what I said, not what I looked like. It was a very gratifying experience.

When I placed the ad, I didn't mention HIV. I figured, I'm not going to open myself up to abuse. My home is my safe place, my haven, and the last thing I want to do is have it invaded via email with vicious types of things. If it came up I would tell people.

One guy in Seattle and I were chatting. We hadn't met in person yet. I had just come back from camping and was sunburned. I said something like, "I go straight from burned to peel." I added, "You're probably one of those people who just tans." He said, "Did I tell you I was black?!" I thought, what the hell. I emailed him back, "Did I tell you I am HIV positive?!" It was hysterical.

I did level with another man I met on the Internet. We actually met face-to-face. After a very pleasant evening I sensed that this relationship could go somewhere. So I told him there was something I had to tell him. His initial response was, "Oh, I have heard this before." He assumed he was getting the boot. And I said, "No, I can guarantee that this is something you haven't heard before." So I told him I became HIV positive in 1993. Initially he was very shocked. Then he did a great recovery and gave me a big hug. Since then we have had some very good times together. Even though it was hard to tell him, I was glad I did.

About my AIDS work, I must admit to having become somewhat burned out. It was emotionally draining. I noticed in my speaking to students that I just lost something. Perhaps I heard it too many times. I also became very disillusioned with my board work because I saw the politics, the cronyism involved, and I frankly just got tired of it. I want to go back to more of a grass-roots level where I actually have contact with people with AIDS. I want to feel that what I do does make a difference.

I CONSIDER MYSELF TO BE EXTREMELY LUCKY. WITH THE EXCEPTION OF ONE INDIVIDUAL, I HAVE NOT HAD TO FACE ON A PERSONAL LEVEL ANY KIND OF PREJUDICE OR BIGOTRY.

JOSEPH JACQUES

Joseph Jacques

I'M A SEVENTY-FIVE-YEAR-OLD psychologist. I do a lot of private and group counseling. I counsel here at the Institute of Human Virology in Baltimore. I also counsel at my home and on the telephone. I lead two support groups for HIV positive people. I want to educate them about HIV infection so they can take care of themselves physically and so they can reduce stress. We do things like biofeedback, guided imagery, meditation, that kind of stuff. I want them to learn about the disease, how to interpret their blood tests, learn what the newest medications and the potential reactions from the newest medications are.

Another role I have is to try to persuade people who are positive to participate in studies here. The Institute is doing immunological studies, and we need people to get involved in that. I do a kind of outreach. I also am a director of a program called the Quality of Life Retreat Program. We do between four and seven retreats a year for HIV positive people. Among the things I discuss is nutrition. I try to teach people how to cook—braising, broiling, steaming, that kind of stuff.

The way we cook is very important. I urge people not to fry food. Many of the people I work with are African Americans and they love fried chicken. They have to give it up because there is too much fat, and because when food is fried, the outside portion of the food is carcinogenic.

When I first became infected, I did as much as I could to learn about this disease. I learned what I could do to reinforce whatever immune system I had left. That led me to all kinds of nutrients, vitamins, and minerals that are helpful to building an immune system. The people in my groups who take supplements are healthier than those who don't. So that makes me feel good.

I was diagnosed in 1985. My doctors and I deduced that I was infected somewhere in the mid-'70s. So I have been infected quite a long time.

I meet lots of young people on the Internet who know what the consequences are of unsafe sex. They do it anyway. And I want to strangle them. I consider what they have done as terribly dumb and idiotic, but I have to help them to survive.

I am a gay man. I used to direct programs and had contact with the judiciary and so on. I always had to be very careful not to be exposed because of my work. Otherwise I would have lost my job probably. So whenever I had a conference to go to, like, Kansas City or Atlanta, I would go to the baths, which turned out to be a very unsafe thing to do. I didn't know about AIDS. If I had known more I wouldn't be positive. It's one of the things I lament.

After my diagnosis, my sexual life just stopped. I haven't had any experiences since 1984. Just abstinence. Well, at the time my doctor intimated that I wouldn't be alive very much longer. I was freaked out but I felt fine. I thought, this is ridiculous. I'm not going to die right away.

I soon became involved with an organization here in Baltimore called Health

Education Resource Center. A friend of mine, a gay man, used to be director of it. That's where I first did my counseling and support groups.

I'm a highly educated person. I have spent twenty-five years of my life in school. The biggest problem for me in the beginning was to talk with people whose education was far beneath mine. I mean, I had to change my whole vocabulary and language. I had to speak at a very low level so that I could be understood. If I was going to help people, I had to be able to communicate with them. So I learned how to do it.

I have saved lots of lives, really. I'm not trying to be egotistical or anything. I have convinced people to change their lifestyles but also helped them to get involved with these natural therapies. I have helped them with their depressions. I have helped them to reduce their stress.

IT IS OFTEN SAID YOU HAVE TO TAKE ONE DAY AT A TIME. WELL, I DON'T BELIEVE THAT. I BELIEVE YOU HAVE TO TAKE ONE DAY AT A TIME AND ALSO CONSIDER THE FUTURE. THERE IS A TOMORROW AND YOU HAVE TO PREPARE FOR THAT. THAT'S WHAT I TRY TO TEACH MY PEOPLE.

Stress is a killer. I know people in my groups who have died of that. They were just so anxious and frightened and unable to relax. I say, "When you feel like you're most relaxed, use your brain to tell your body what to do."

My health is generally quite good, except for neuropathy, which has affected my feet and legs. The nerves there are gone, so I can't sense balance and I fall. This is the consequence of all the drugs I'm on. All of the problems I have are the result of treatment. That's one of the things I lament. I'm a believer, as this Institute is, in the immune system. I'm sorry I didn't give my immune system a chance to beat this without using drugs.

I'm in a study about nerve growth that is being done at [Johns] Hopkins. I have to inject myself twice a week. I have been doing that for three and a half years. It seems to be helpful, but it's very slow. The tingling is the beginning, the numbness follows the tingling, and then when it gets to be very advanced it's very painful, almost unbearable. I also have diarrhea from the protease I'm on. So my legs hurt and I hurt on my rear end. I have learned to survive with pain.

I don't think I will be here for a cure even though my family has very good genes. But what I hope for is something that will enable me to get off the proteases so I can eliminate the diarrhea and to find some sort of cure for the neuropathy. If those things were eliminated in my life, my life would be much more productive than I am now and much happier. I am very busy, but I could do a lot more if I didn't have these pains.

I'm a Christian. Jesus asked us all to serve, and that's what I do. I admire the life of Christ and try to emulate it if I can. I was raised a Catholic. No, I don't go to church. The only time I go to a church is to look at the paintings.

I get support from the people that I support. We love each other and they know when I need a rest. We understand how important we are to each other. As for any other personal support, I don't have any close friends, except for Dr. Redfield. He's my doctor and has been very helpful to me. I love him. He's a compassionate man and he's an excellent clinician. We've done things for each other, and I do regard him as a very close friend. Since he's my doctor, though, I find it a little bit more difficult to be a friend.

My family doesn't know I am HIV positive. If I told my eighty-five-year-old brother or my eighty-nine-year-old sister that I was sick and that I was a gay person, they would freak out.

I'm on the computer a lot. Most of the time it's for research. Before computers I went to libraries. I access a number of Web sites that describe the newest HIV research. I make copies for all the people who work here at the Institute. I make a judgment about which research articles are important. They appreciate it.

I also use the Internet for answering questions that come up in chat rooms. There are a number of gay and HIV chat rooms. I wake up two or three times a night and I go to the chat rooms, sometimes at 2 A.M. Otherwise it's impossible to get on, it's so busy. One of the most common problems that comes up is a gay man is married, has children, he and his wife are miserable because their sex life is miserable. And so we talk and I try to help him.

With the people I counsel, the long-term goal is to make them understand that they have a future, that they aren't going to die from AIDS. I want them to gain skills that will enable them not only to survive but to produce something. If they are women with children, to enable them to take care of those children with ease, not having to depend on anybody else to take care of them. If they are single women or men, to convince them they are able to work. And that they should go out and find jobs. Or to get into some rehabilitation program to go back to school. It is often said you have to take one day at a time. Well, I don't believe that. I believe you have to take one day at a time and also consider the future. There is a tomorrow and you have to prepare for that. That's what I try to teach my people.

I'm an old guy and I have all sorts of problems. My purpose is to continue to stay alive. I don't have any particular goals other than to try to help people. I mean, I have done everything in my life that I think I want to do. There are things I would have liked to have done, like more traveling. I have lots of friends in Europe that I haven't been able to see. With my neuropathy, it's too difficult. Of course I am interested in continuing to learn. I think when you stop learning, you're dead.

[UPDATE]

Joseph Jacques died eight months after this interview.

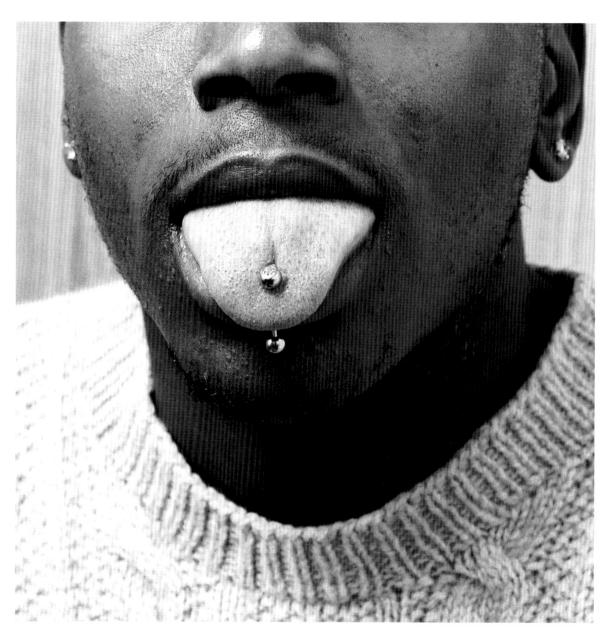

J A E V A U G H N

Jaevaughn

I AM EIGHTEEN years old. I was seventeen when I found out I was HIV positive. What happened was in August 1999, I was raped by a boyfriend of mine. I took a test and found out I was positive.

I didn't tell anyone. I kept it inside. I broke up with the boyfriend after he had raped me. I saw doctors at Mt. Sinai's Adolescent Health Clinic in New York. I just started taking medication. It made me physically ill. I couldn't function at school. I lost almost sixty pounds. I started throwing up. I had diarrhea, chronic fatigue all the time. So I stopped going to school. After I had missed three months of school, I couldn't go back. I didn't want to go back because I missed too much to catch up.

My mother is a nurse. I didn't tell my mother about my diagnosis for more than half a year. I couldn't tell her because she always seemed to be anti-gay. To this day she says it's not the case. So I finally told her all at once. I told her I was gay. I told her I was positive. It was a whole big thing. She was going through things with her own personal life. She gave me a hard time about how long I took to tell her. In all honesty she reacted different from how I imagined. She was very supportive. "Just take care of yourself. Eat nice food." She wants to help me. I suppose she always did. I had an uncle who died of AIDS. When my uncle died, it affected my whole family because he was really a key figure. He was a gay man. I was very close to him. He was like a mentor to me, just like a second father. I knew about AIDS from him, so I tried my whole life not to put myself at risk, like having unprotected sex, stuff like that.

I DIDN'T TELL MY MOTHER ABOUT MY DIAGNOSIS FOR MORE THAN HALF A YEAR. I COULDN'T TELL HER BECAUSE SHE ALWAYS SEEMED TO BE ANTI-GAY. TO THIS DAY SHE SAYS IT'S NOT THE CASE. SO I FINALLY TOLD HER ALL AT ONCE. I TOLD HER I WAS GAY. I TOLD HER I WAS POSITIVE. IT WAS A WHOLE BIG THING.

After my diagnosis I left home. I didn't want to comply with my mother's rules. So I left. I have lived in a group home now, a "safe home."

There are ten of us there. We are all positive. I have my own clique inside the house. Outside the house I have my best friend and a few other friends. I am very discreet about who I call a friend. My best friend does not know I am positive. I do not want to tell him because he is not a strong person. We grew up in Brooklyn together.

I only dated two people since I was positive. I told them both I was positive at the very beginning. Not the first date but the first two weeks. I hoped that I could trust them and that they would understand. So I just come out and say it because I'm a strong person. It's wrong to wait for a while before you tell somebody you're HIV positive. It's hurtful.

Now I'm on the same medicines as I was in the beginning when I was throwing up. My doctors said I was reading too much. I was having the side effects I was reading about. So I've stopped reading and things have settled down.

I'm about to get my GED. I want to start college in January and get a job. I want to be a psychiatric social worker. I'm planning on majoring in psychology and minoring in sociology.

I wish to be successful in my relationships and in life—to stop being so jealous and to learn that the world does not revolve around me. I also would like to be married someday. I could go to Vermont for a same-sex marriage. I feel that as long as you are committed to each other and you trust each other and you connect mentally, physically, spiritually, then that's marriage. If you connect on those different levels, then there's no reason why the relationship can't last. To say I am married, to have that ring on my finger, would be a different feeling from other relationships.

I would like to live in France, in a place southwest of Paris. I have been there. I went there with my family not too long ago. My father was from Haiti. He died in 1989. My mother is from Barbados. Growing up we spoke French and English at home. I love languages.

My ex-boyfriend made me get this tongue ring. No, it didn't hurt. At first I was reluctant to do it but I did it anyway. It symbolizes our relationship. I have my birthstone and his birthstone at each end of the ring. We're still friends and I still love him and even though he is my "ex" I think we'll be back together again.

PAULA PETERSON AND GRIFF BUTLER

WITH BEN

Paula Peterson
and Griff Butler

PAULA PETERSON

WHEN I FIRST LEARNED that I had full-blown AIDS, I thought I was going to die the next day. I felt like my future had been cut off. That was nine or ten months ago. Time now is broken up into "before the diagnosis" and "after the diagnosis." Every day is really weighty. Rather than months, I feel it in days. It just feels like every hour, every minute counts. It's not that I feel that I don't have a future exactly. It's just very uncertain. But I no longer wake up and think I am going to die that day.

It took a long time before I was diagnosed with AIDS. I was very run-down after the baby was born. I was tired—but all new mothers are tired. Then I got very sick with sinusitis. I had very high fevers, night sweats. The doctor gave me antibiotics. But I just really didn't get better. Then I developed a nasty ear infection. And I had an awful cough. I had lost weight. At that point I was beginning to think, there is something going on here.

I kept going back and forth to doctors and nurse practitioners at a major hospital. They even did a pulmonary function test and CT scans of my head. They did various blood tests. Nothing showed up. But they did not give me an HIV test. I remember one doctor who said, "Well, do you think you are depressed?" And I said, "Yeah, I'm really depressed because I've been sick for so long." Finally four months later my doctor said, "Why don't you take an HIV test? You don't have anything that would lead me to think you had AIDS, but why don't you try it to rule it out?"

I really didn't think AIDS was a possibility, but I was still really frightened of the test. I had an appointment with my doctor two weeks after the test. I remember trying to call his office before the two weeks to find out the test results. I spoke to a nurse who said, "Oh, don't worry about it. Just wait to see your doctor." And so I finally saw my doctor at the scheduled appointment. I had to remind him I was waiting for the results of my HIV test. He went out of the room and came back and said, "I have some really harsh news for you." And that's how I found out.

My husband and my son were tested. I was very worried about my son because I breast-fed him up until the morning of my diagnosis. They showed up negative. That is a miracle! How I got AIDS remains a mystery. I have been with my husband basically since 1989. I contacted boyfriends I had before my marriage and they are fine. And I know it wasn't drugs. It's kind of a mystery I have to let go of.

I was such a basket case when I was first diagnosed that I really don't know how I pulled myself out of it. I think it was taking care of my son that helped me. I realized I had to be a mother to him again and that was one thing that helped get me off the couch. And then, of course, gradually having my physical strength return and doing well on the medications that were given to me. I've been on the protease inhibitors and I've done very well on them. I'm really feeling almost like my old self.

I think I have always had some inner strength. I've never had to go through anything as bad as this in my life. But I haven't fallen apart either. I love to read. I write. I've been going to a therapist once a week and that helps.

My husband has been really wonderful. And my parents were supportive from the beginning. At first my mother was in a state of shock, of course, especially when I didn't know if my baby was sick. That was the hardest thing to go through, the first couple of weeks before we knew my son's test results. My parents moved from the Midwest to be closer to me so they could help out. When I first got diagnosed, they were here almost every day. I was also very depressed, just out of my mind with worry. So they really were helping me. But it's hard for them to live here. It's not their hometown and they feel out of place.

Now I feel healthy again, and I am able to take care of my son myself. I've also been reaching out to people more and have started to make some friends here. Just having a baby helped. I know other women with babies. They don't have HIV, but they have all been very supportive of me. I don't have any close friends with AIDS that I can share this with. That part is missing in my life right now.

FOR ME TO DARE TO MAKE PLANS FOR THE FUTURE IS REMARKABLE. I HAD BARELY STARTED DREAMING AND MAKING PLANS ABOUT MY SON WHEN I GOT SICK. SO MAYBE THE THINGS I AM DREAMING ABOUT ARE WHAT EVERY MOTHER DREAMS ABOUT.

For me to dare to make plans for the future is remarkable. I had barely started dreaming and making plans about my son when I got sick. So maybe the things I am dreaming about are what every mother dreams about. My husband and I both love to hike. So we dream of the day when our son is old enough to backpack. I dream about teaching him to read and to love books. But I think that would have always been there too, illness or no illness. I've been discussing what schools are best for my son. We are making plans for a vacation. We're talking about buying a house. Just normal everyday plans. Things that families do. I just try to live like I always did live, pre-diagnosis.

When I look back on what happened to me, what caused my "downfall," it was just ignorance, thinking that someone like me couldn't get this disease. "A nice, white, middle-class girl can't get HIV!" That's why the doctors didn't suggest earlier that I be tested. But even if you aren't a drug user or a gay man, you can get HIV. I believe that pregnant women should be tested routinely. There are things they can do now for pregnant women with HIV. I was very lucky with Benjamin. And he got lucky. The fact that I had a C-section helped protect him, even though at the time I hated giving birth this way.

If I had known I was sick, I don't think I would have made the choice to have a child. So I feel lucky that I have a son and that he is healthy. I guess my biggest fear is that he won't know me. That I won't be alive long enough for him to really know me. And so that makes me more determined to stay well.

[FOUR YEARS LATER]

It has been five years since I was diagnosed. Although in many ways my life has remained the same, from an emotional and psychological perspective I am light-years away from the woman I was then. In those years my health has improved immensely. My T cells hover between 500 and 600, which is considered to be a normal range and puts me out of the danger zone for opportunistic infections, and my viral load has remained undetectable. I've switched to a protease inhibitor that is easier to take. Aside from that, my combination is basically the same. I'm lucky. I haven't had any serious illnesses and I live a virtually normal life, except for the fact that I have to take drugs every day and go to the doctor frequently.

The only real physical complaint I have right now is cosmetic—my body has changed in some drastic ways due to a peculiar side effect of the drugs called lipodystrophy, a condition that affects the way fat is distributed on the body. My arms and legs are much more wasted than what you see in the photograph from 1997, my face is thinner, and my waist is thicker. There's not much I can do about this, and I suppose I'm lucky because I don't have the internal correlates that often go along with this condition— high lipid and cholesterol levels, or in some cases diabetes. I feel ashamed of being so vain, and I know I should be grateful just to be alive and healthy and forget about my looks, but I can't help it! Every time I look at that first picture I long for my fuller face and more youthful appearance—even though I'm much healthier now than I was then, appearances notwithstanding.

I've changed in other ways besides the physical. Nowadays I consider myself to be a part of mainstream life—meaning that I don't feel as isolated by my disease and I feel I can participate in almost anything that negative people can do. In fact, I'm proud of the fact that I'm in much better shape than some of my negative friends! I assume, like everybody else, that I will live to see my child grow up, and that I have work to do in the world, that I have something valuable to contribute, that I can be productive and not just a burden to society. Whether my assumptions are ill founded or not, only time will tell, but I think it is healthy to live this way.

The most essential aspect of my existence boils down to two things: raising my child and writing. And I do plenty of time on both fronts. Ben is a happy, healthy, well-adjusted six-year-old boy, very intelligent and active and curious. I've grown to love being home with him. I wouldn't have missed these years, although if you had asked me what I thought of stay-at-home mothers before he was born, I would have replied contemptuously. Being forced to stay home because of HIV helped me to see what was most meaningful for me. I don't feel at all guilty about still being on disability. I've made a lot of valuable use of my time, so I don't feel I've been wasting the government's money.

The other main part of my life is my writing. In the last five years I've become much more disciplined about my craft, much more focused on it. Again, HIV may have played a part here—I feel more of an urgency to write, more aware of death. And having a child constricts you a bit, too, forces you to keep more regular habits. So I credit Ben a lot in turning me into a "real" writer.

I just had my first book published, *Penitent, with Roses: An HIV+ Mother Reflects*

[University Press of New England, 2001], and I have a new collection of short stories about HIV positive mothers which I'm hoping to get published. I have all sorts of long-term plans as a writer. I don't intend to always write about HIV either. One of the luxuries of being healthy now is that I feel I can branch out to other topics—take my place in the literary community, in other words, as I've taken my place in the parenting community.

I've changed in other ways, too. In the last five years I've done lots of volunteer work, including working on the San Francisco AIDS Foundation hotline and lobbying in Washington, D.C. I also have just started tutoring kids to read, and I work at my son's school. It's funny. This urge to give back, to contribute, happens to a lot of people with HIV. It's not that I consider myself a "do-gooder." I'm still mainly a selfish type—you have to be when you're a writer—but for some mysterious reason I found myself attracted to volunteering.

IT HAS BEEN FIVE YEARS SINCE I WAS DIAGNOSED. ALTHOUGH IN MANY WAYS MY LIFE HAS REMAINED THE SAME, FROM AN EMOTIONAL AND PSYCHOLOGICAL PERSPECTIVE I AM LIGHT-YEARS AWAY FROM THE WOMAN I WAS THEN.

I still get depressed from time to time. I can be compulsive, too, a big worrier, and I get irritated about petty things. I suffer doubly when I'm in a bad mood because I feel guilty about the depression. I feel like since I've been granted this miracle of good health, I should be grateful and make good use of my time, not waste a moment. I was talking with another HIV positive friend of mine recently about this pressure to live in an elevated or a particularly evolved way. That's part of the myth of being seriously ill, that we turn into saints somehow. And of course we don't.

Essentially, though, I'm a joyful person, and I'm ambitious, too. I don't feel like a "cursed" person like I did five years ago. When that picture was taken in 1997, I was standing precariously on the sidelines of life, waiting to see what would happen to me and trying to hold myself together. Now I feel like a full-fledged participant, and that means I fail or succeed in ways that are much like everybody else, that sometimes I'm good at living and sometimes I'm not. I like not being so "special" anymore. I like having the same chances everybody else does.

I am a systems analyst for an airline. The good thing about my job is that it gives me a chance to get my mind off everything. I am sure I have kept my feelings internal.

Through the years I had been tested pretty regularly when I gave blood. I always thought, well, I'm not in the statistical group and I don't do anal sex. So I wasn't really worried. I didn't think it was possible for Paula to be sick either, so we were both in a state of shock when she got her diagnosis.

It's been very tough having Paula sick and having a baby. It's hard to rest when you have a baby. I'm up a lot in the night taking care of Ben, because Paula can't do it. Stuff really frazzles me now. Like the other day I spilled something in the fridge and I just went off. Usually I'm very easygoing. It's a combination of the sickness, taking care of Benjamin, and then having to deal with Paula's parents. It makes it rough. Dealing with these things sort of diverts me from what I should be concerned about, which is Paula's health.

Paula and I never used to bicker, but we bicker a lot now over simple stuff. Paula was saying to me, "You'd better go to a counselor. You're stressed out."

I went to a support group for caregivers and basically it was for people who are right near the end. The group I was in, everyone was gay. It was sort of scary because before going to this group I had thought, well, we have these protease inhibitors and everything is fine. She might not feel her best but everything will go on. In this support group, two people died that were on the protease inhibitors. And two others had partners who had dementia. Whoa! So actually, I didn't tell her what was going on when I went to these meetings. These people were in advanced stages of dementia and we're talking about going on vacation and I'm thinking, "This could be happening soon." I've tried not to think about that. It might be easier if Benjamin was older.

IT SORT OF PUTS A DAMPER ON THE SEX DRIVE WHEN YOU KNOW THAT WITH ONE MIS-TAKE YOU CAN GET AIDS. WHAT CAN YOU SAY?

We went to this other group and there were some gay guys in there. We asked them, "What do you do? Who do you contact?" They were surprised that we didn't know other people with AIDS and that we didn't know about any resources. But now Paula has found a group of heterosexuals that are HIV positive. That's good for her. It's sort of a singles group though. There aren't many couples where one is positive and one is negative.

Sometimes I think if we didn't have a child, the easy thing to do would be to say, "Hey, I can't handle this" and forget it. But I haven't even thought about that. I'm sort of focused on raising Benjamin, so I'm not dwelling on all these other things. I shouldn't get mad. I just have this internal anger that I blow up over little things around the house.

Benjamin is starting to talk now. I'm looking forward to ages three to eight or so. From seeing my niece and nephew, those seem to be the fun years. I don't know how he's going to deal with the fact, once he learns his mother has AIDS. I don't know if there's a stigma anymore when your mom has AIDS—probably not in San Francisco. In Indiana there might be.

It's been a problem for us sexually. It sort of puts a damper on the sex drive when you know that with one mistake you can get AIDS. What can you say? We still have sex but nowhere near like what we used to. Condoms can break. There are dental dams for oral sex and all that. Chances are nothing is going to happen, but if something does happen, you can get AIDS. Really the only safe way is just to abstain. I don't know if that's an option.

My father and grandmother died of cancer. It was a two-year process. My father was two hundred pounds and he ended up about seventy or eighty pounds when he finally died. Going through that process, you just learn to deal with it. In the AIDS support group I was telling them ways of going forward. It's almost like numbing your mind to what is going on. Some of these people never had anyone die they were close to and they couldn't come to grips with it.

I guess I'm just going on a day at a time. We're in a book group. In fact, I'm going tomorrow night. A few sessions ago Paula just came out and told everyone that she has AIDS. It made everyone quiet. It pretty much ended that book group meeting. This couple said they were just bummed out thinking about the stuff Paula and I are going through. So I'm not even thinking about all that stuff. I'm glad that Paula is OK. They keep coming out with new drugs, so I'm not expecting anything to happen anytime soon.

STEPHANIE RHODES

Stephanie Rhodes

I AM AN INCEST SURVIVOR. When I was growing up I was a battered child, an abused child. And so that made me very angry on the inside. Having all that anger and frustration and bad feelings and not knowing where to put them, I just stayed to myself and I read.

What eventually happened is that I met somebody when I was in high school. And this person said he was abused by his mother and so he knew exactly how I felt. I started spending a lot of time with him and I stopped going to school. I never knew what love was. Nobody had ever kissed me or told me that they loved me. I married this person when I was eighteen. He was two years older than I was. I got pregnant toward the latter part of the eleventh grade. And that was the first time I ever gave myself to somebody. This person said that's the way you show love. And I had the child. And then I got pregnant with another. He wanted me to have an abortion, but I didn't believe in abortions.

Me and him, we didn't get together too much because he, as I like to call him, turned out to be a negroid version of Adolph Hitler. He was a really bad person. I was a battered wife, and I ended up going to about twenty-three different battered women shelters.

I retreated back into my mind. There wasn't anything but pain there. Where I come from my father said, "Black people don't see psychiatrists. Only white people do." Because the black people work out their problems at home.

I moved to Oakland when I was twenty-five or twenty-six. That's where my life became very distorted. I had memories of being sodomized and people raping me from the time I was three. So I was in my own private little hell.

My mother left when I was a baby. My father and my stepmother abused me—my father because he knew what was going on and told us not to do anything about it, and my stepmother who perpetrated a lot of things. Like she would take money from men to have sex with me when I was three years old. My stepmother didn't tell my father that men paid her to come over and have sex with me during their lunch hour but she told him, "Rufus dropped by." I had to go to the doctor all the time. If that was my child, I would have asked, "Why does she have to go to the doctor all the time?" My stepmother would hit me and make me fall and trip and burn me with cigarettes and my father didn't do anything about that either.

By the time I was twenty-seven I started using drugs. I used to see this guy at the store and he would just see me sad. And then he asked me if I wanted to try something that would make me feel better. And he gave me some crack and I stayed on crack for the next eight years. It gave me this really euphoric feeling and I didn't have any memories or bad thoughts and I could smile and I was OK and the world was OK and life was OK. And so I tried to get as much crack as I could.

I gave my children up to their father, which is the worst thing I could have ever done. No, the worst thing I could have done was to take crack, but I didn't know that then. In the eighth year of crack, I didn't know how to stop. I was homeless. I met this person that told me about Narcotics Anonymous and Alcoholics Anonymous. At first I thought I could stop using drugs by myself, just like not going to a psychiatrist—you handle it, you just stop and stay committed to stop. And I would stop. But after three or four months I was back there in the same situation.

So I called the guy who had told me about NA and he came with me to my first NA meeting. It wasn't easy. I kept relapsing. But I have been clean for three and a half years. I was thirty-two when I was introduced to NA and now I am thirty-six.

Right now, my social worker is going to help get my son back. He is fourteen. My daughters are eighteen and seventeen. I also have a seven-year-old daughter. Right now she is in a foster home. I get her every weekend like I get my fourteen-year-old son every weekend. And they are going to give me back custody of my son. Now I am going to fight for my daughter, which shouldn't be no problem because I've been coming to get her every weekend

WHEN YOU ARE HIV POSITIVE, YOU TAKE ON ANOTHER JOB LOOKING AFTER YOUR MEDICATIONS. I USED TO DO COMPUTER REPAIR. I WAS A FIELD SERVICE TECH AND WOULD GO TO DIFFERENT COMPANIES AND REPAIR FAX MACHINES AND STUFF. THAT JOB AIN'T NOTHING COMPARED TO BEING HIV POSITIVE AND TRYING TO TAKE YOUR MEDICATIONS WHEN YOU ARE SUPPOSED TO TAKE THEM.

religiously for the past two years. She wants to be with me. I went through a whole lot of things—parenting classes. I've been going to see a therapist for about five years. I have been seeing a psychiatrist for about two and a half years.

One of the things that I would really want people to know, I was never a promiscuous person. Never, ever a promiscuous person. The way I got HIV is that I would have sex with this guy and he would give me drugs. And that was the only person I was sexually involved with. But we used two condoms. I thought that was extra safe. What I found out is that two condoms together serve as friction against each other, and that makes them tear faster. Just the opposite from being extra safe.

I found out I was positive five years ago. After I had it for six months, I got neuropathy in my feet, my knees, my hips, and the base of my spine. Neuropathy means my nerve endings are dying. That means at some point I won't be able to walk anymore. It is getting worse. I am in pain all the time.

I take twelve different medications—for pain, for ulcers, so I can sleep, for migraine, for blood pressure, for moods. The thing is that I have had such a troubled past, and I have all these bad memories. They come into my brain and turn themselves into physical images. So I take different things to help me stay in the moment, is the best way I could put it.

When you are HIV positive, you take on another job looking after your medications. I used to do computer repair. I was a field service tech and would go to different companies and repair fax machines and stuff. That job ain't nothing compared to being HIV positive and trying to take your medications when you are supposed to take them.

I've had a fiancé person for five years. He is my support. And then Social Services Department is there when I have problems. I can call them and they'll come. They will clean me up, bathe me or cook or do the laundry or vacuum or whatever is necessary. My fiancé person has a pager and I can call him. Sometimes he can take me to the bathroom when I need to throw up and help clean it up or whatever. When he gets off of work, a lot of times he comes over here and checks on me. He is a good person. He doesn't have HIV or anything.

I used to worry about giving him HIV. I don't worry too much about it now. He's eleven years older than I am and he's a big boy and he knows what he wants to do and what he can't do. We use prophylactics at more intimate times.

Sometimes I go out by myself if I am having a good day. I go to Project Open Hand every week. I like to go and pick my own stuff out. My fiancé person generally takes one day off a week, and he'll take me up there. They give you enough food to supplement what you already have.

The thing is, I have never been a pitiful person. I have never had to ask people to help with my daily functions, to help feed or clothe my family or to take care of me. I have always been an independent person and it bothers me to no avail, this HIV, because I often need help. I'm a control freak, but when I am sick I can control nothing. I can't even move my head sometimes. I don't want nobody to help me unless I absolutely have to. I may really need help someday and I don't want somebody to just throw me around because they're tired of helping.

I have a God. He talks to me. He tells me when the bus is coming. He tells me when the cab is not going to come.

Me and my mother, we didn't used to have a real good relationship. She's in Texas now. I see her about every two years. I let her know about my HIV, and I give my children a briefing about four times a year, all except the seven-year-old.

My mother wants me to come down to Texas and be with her. But she knows that San Francisco has more medical options that they can offer me. If it ever came to a point where I wasn't going to get any better, then she would be the first one to say, "Put her on a plane, bring her over."

For my own kids, I do encourage schooling and reading. With your education you don't have to look at that pretty little car in the magazine. If you go to school and get a job, you can buy that pretty little car. When my children come visit me, they don't just sit and watch TV. We bake cookies. We read. We draw and write. I like to draw. I like to listen to music loudly. I like rhythm and blues and oldies. And I like to clean up my house.

I don't dream for myself. To be honest, I don't have a future. I want to be there to show my children the importance of education, to teach them African American history, and to let them know the meaning behind the word *no*. I want to be there to give my seven-year-old self-confidence, to teach her to love herself. I want to be near my fiancé person I love one day at a time.

DIERRO   MUNIZ

Dierro Muniz

MY PARENTS were born in San Antonio. My father's family were sharecroppers. He was able to get out of sharecropping. He had a very good fender and body business. From that he and my mother built some Mexican restaurants.

I grew up in Mineral Wells, a small town on the west side of Fort Worth, Texas. Approximately twenty thousand people lived there, predominantly white, although now there is a big influx of immigrants.

Texas is extremely conservative. I felt like I had a lot of difficulties being in two minorities, one being a Mexican American and the other being gay. Growing up, my parents always knew I was gay but it was never discussed. Eventually I told my parents, a year after I was diagnosed, when I was thirty-two. I have one sister who has children. We're very close.

There were some difficult moments growing up in Texas, but I have told my dad that I wouldn't change my life for anything else. The minorities would stick together and they wouldn't blend with the good ol' white boys. And now when I go back a lot of guys look at me. They are attracted to me and I just feel the difference. In 1982, when I was coming out, it wasn't like that. But things have changed in twenty years.

I went from Mineral Wells to the University of Texas in Austin, graduating with a degree in civil engineering. Late '87 I was recruited by an engineering firm and moved to Boston, where I worked for a construction management company. We did large-scale commercial construction downtown. At that time Boston was experiencing a boom time. Compared to Texas, Boston was a much more liberal environment.

I FEEL LIKE THIS ILLNESS IN ONE WAY IS BITTERSWEET. . . . WHEN I GOT DIAGNOSED, IT COST ME MY CAREER AT ITS HEIGHT. I FEEL CHEATED. . . . ON THE OTHER HAND, I HAVE BEEN ABLE TO REST AND SPEND MORE TIME WITH MY FAMILY, MY SISTER, MY PARENTS, AND MY NIECE AND NEPHEW, SO IT'S A TRADE-OFF. . . . BEFORE MY DIAGNOSIS, I WAS THE TYPE WHO WOULD NEVER STOP TO SMELL THE ROSES.

In 1988, after I was diagnosed with HIV, I continued working for three years for this company and finally decided the tail was wagging the dog. It just became very difficult with trying to manage doctors appointments. I became involved with a couple of studies, clinical trials, at Beth Israel Deaconess Hospital. Being in the studies required a lot of time.

The Deaconess had a night clinic at the time for people who were working. So you could come in at night, see your doctor at 6 P.M., have your blood drawn at 7 and go home. I would go home and barely have enough time to touch up a shirt. And then back at work at 7 A.M. the next day. It was just too much.

I didn't tell anybody at work about my status. Naturally disclosure was a very scary thing, especially in a construction environment, where I think they are more conservative. I finally disclosed my situation when I told them I had to quit. They were so supportive, especially my boss, who is a Baptist Bible beater. I thought he would slam the door when I told him. But do you know, he still calls me to this day and wants to know how my T cells are and how I am feeling. He has been a true Christian. That made me so proud to be a part of their work team.

I finally quit working in 1990 and went on disability. I got involved with acupuncture, Chinese herbs, massage, and psychotherapy. And I worked out. A very important part of my life was the Mind/Body support group connected to the Deaconess Hospital, run by Dr. Ann Webster. We learned how to relax and how to cope through meditation and other techniques. Besides saving my life the group gave me the companionship of other people and showed me that I wasn't by myself. It was very difficult because there were funerals every month. We would all look at each other and wonder who was going to be next.

When I was first diagnosed, AZT was the only drug available to the public. I was very lucky I was able to get on clinical trials, because once the AZT started to fail me after a year, there would have been nothing else. New drugs became available through the studies. Every year I was able to get one year ahead of the game, which I think was just enough time to save my life.

My health continued to decline through the early '90s. On Christmas of '95 I was hospitalized for an infection on my leg . When I came out of that I had only fourteen T cells—a normal person has approximately one thousand—so I was in a very critical stage. I was trying to get on the protease inhibitors. We were all aware of them for almost all of 1995. However, any kind of compassionate use or studies required that the person had to have at least fifty T cells. In the early part of 1996, in January, they came out with the very first protease inhibitor through Abbott Laboratories. I got it right away. Within the first six weeks my viral load was zero. It was a complete turn-around. Everything was back on the upward spiral, although it was a very slow climb.

The chemistry of the support group was changing because the whole face of the disease was changing. Early on we talked about going on disability, starting our very first drug regimen, getting our wills and funerals together. With the new protease inhibitors all of a sudden there was hope, actually a future. We started talking about how we needed to start saving money and quit spending our assets. I myself had sold some property that I had with my sister.

In 1998 I moved from Boston to Hollywood, California. I wanted to turn a page in my book. I also wanted to move there to have friends who didn't know about my HIV. It's not as if I'm ashamed about what has happened to me. But I just don't want to talk about it. In Boston almost every conversation revolved around HIV, medications, etcetera. And that was a good thing when it happened. I needed that. But that was then. Now I want to have some friends who don't know anything about my health and we will be able to talk about other things. I think that's kind of healthy. There is a big community in Los Angeles of people who are positive, and I have made some positive friends too. But I don't want to get completely wrapped up in the HIV world twenty-four hours a day.

When I moved to California I was going to try restart my career. I haven't gone back to work yet, but that is my focus. I want to do it slowly and carefully because my T cells are the highest count I have ever had, 310. I want to get further away from 200 because 200 is kind of the mark where you have to start certain prophylactic medications for pneumonia and other things. I know what stress can do.

I was lucky to have a good disability insurance policy that pays 67 percent of what my salary was as an engineer. It allowed me not to worry about anything. The minute I start generating income I will lose that. Unfortunately, the way the laws are, once I am off the disability I can't get back on. But there are now laws that require insurance companies to include people with HIV, especially if you go in on a group policy. But there are certain clauses, depending on the policy, like six-month predisposition clauses and that kind of thing.

I feel like this illness in one way is bittersweet. I feel like I survived it even though there is a small possibility that something can go wrong. I feel that it did several things for me, both professionally and emotionally. When I got diagnosed, it cost me my career at its height. I feel cheated. But that's OK because I would rather have my life. On the other hand, I have been able to rest and spend more time with my family, my sister, my parents, and my niece and nephew, so it's a trade-off. My parents told me they pray for me.

Before my diagnosis, I was the type who would never stop to smell the roses. From 7 A.M. to 10 at night, it was always business, business, business.

I was involved with Richard for seven years. He's negative. When we first met I had not been diagnosed. For the most part he did go through it with me. He left me in '95 when I needed him the most. When I look back at all the people who helped save my life, he was one of them.

I haven't had a serious relationship since. It's been heavy on my mind. I don't know why exactly I can't meet anybody that I am interested in. When I think of dreams, I think of developing a good relationship with another man that could be long lasting. Because I have more free time and my health has been consistently good, I'm starting to feel I can rededicate myself to my career and finding a boyfriend. I go to the Gold's Gym and I work out five days a week. I try make a lot of my own food. I drink a lot of protein shakes and take a lot of vitamins. I am looking forward to going back to work. You know, I'm kind of ready for it.

BERNARD PECHTER

Bernard Pechter

MY FAMILY'S first language was Yiddish and the second was Polish. My father, a tinsmith, conducted his business in Polish. We lived behind the stockyards in Chicago. I was one of the two rebels in the family.

Chicago was singularly the most oppressive place in the world. It was the time of Mayor Richard Daley the First. I had a really hard time growing up in that I knew I was different. I didn't know where to go, so I used to cruise public restrooms. I got arrested once and had to spend the night in jail. No, I didn't know I was gay. I knew I was strange. I knew whatever I was doing was wrong.

I still resent the new young people talking about "queers." That's the new word for gays by gays. It's like blacks calling each other "niggers." Last year's parade was called "Queer, Lesbian, Bisexual, Transgender." Well, I won't support that because I thought of myself as a queer and I knew that was wrong.

I left Chicago when I was seventeen, went away to school, worked for a while, and then came to San Francisco in 1959. The degree of openness in San Francisco was like no place I had ever been to. Sure, there was entrapment and the usual kind of thing. Sure, they used to raid the bars, but it wasn't as bad as Chicago and New York. In those days I wouldn't have dreamed of going to the opera without taking a woman. We used to call them "appliances"—we'd plug them in to go. Still, some men showed up with their boyfriends. I just wasn't one of them.

For the next twenty-three years I pissed away most of my money in psychoanalysis. I spent four days a week on a couch trying to change from gay to straight. It wasn't even "gay" then, it was "homosexual."

In those early days of living in California, I was teaching Italian and working on a master's in comparative literature. I was a good teacher and a terrible scholar. In the end I decided not to be an academic. One day I went to a job interview at a stockbrokerage—I knew a lot about Dante and nothing about stockbrokerages. But I got hired as a trainee. It was the best six months of my life.

I became a stockbroker and slowly built a clientele, pretty much people in the entertainment business and some academics. I wasn't the type that was going to deal with CPAs and attorneys. I was a good salesman. I would look for a stock and sell it all day long. In those days the market was like minting money.

I was the first person to publicly go after the gay market. I knew a lot of rich gays. The New York Stock Exchange allowed me to put an ad in the *Advocate* saying, "How to make money in Levis." What gay man didn't have a pair of Levis, the sexiest thing? Levis had just become a public corporation, so you could buy stock. Suddenly I had accounts coming out of my ears, not just from the States but from all over the world.

In the mid-1980s I really was burned out. I got involved in drugs at a very late age, and the drugs took over my life. I found amphetamines—that is probably the most popular drug among gays even today—and ran with it. In the course of that it ruined a business, a life, a great deal of things. I lost a home that I built on the most beautiful street in San Francisco. I lost a major art collection including Diebenkorn and Motherwell. After trying unsuccessfully to get my life back, I finally went to a place called Pride, which is a recovery center for gays and lesbians in Minnesota. It did make a difference.

I was really shocked when I discovered I had HIV two years ago. And it's only now that I am beginning to tell people of my circumstances. My closest cousins in California think I have a communicable, airborne disease. They have little to do with me now that I told them. I also don't want my brother to know. He is going to be seventy-five and he just had open heart surgery. As a gay person you have to create your own family.

I have a lot of fears about what's going to happen to me, losing control and who is going to be there for me. I don't know if I can count on anybody. And that's something I'm working out with my AIDS counselor at Jewish Family Services. Much of my support comes from her.

One of my great passions is baseball. In grammar school I used to cut school all the time to go to Cubs games. In 1966 I had an epiphany and I converted from Cubs to Giants. Now, during baseball season, I go to almost all the home games.

I started out poor, I've been rich, and now I'm poor again, living on Social Security. That means I can't make more than $100 a week. I have a little job now working at a brokerage firm doing miscellaneous stuff. I work generally from 9 to 12, then I have lunch, and if I'm feeling well, I go to the gym. I have neuropathy in my feet, so it's very difficult for me to walk.

I went to Shanti and they matched me with a volunteer and she is just perfect. She has a quality that I haven't seen very often in my life with women. All the others have been much more like my mother, ball busters, but my volunteer gives me compassion, warmth, caring. She's really a cause of my wellness and the reason I really want to go on. We talk every day no matter where I am, even when I go away. She's wonderful company. We go to opera and theater together. And she takes me shopping. If I become incontinent, and I have to tell you it's terribly embarrassing, I know I can call her and she will make me feel better. She has a way of turning it around. She loves to love. She has this magic laugh. And I like to make her laugh. She is what we call a "fucking jewel."

Right now I don't have that many gay friends left. They've all died. Last Thursday one of my closest friends, Frank, died, and I was pleased he was "spared." This is a holocaust. There is no sense to the deaths. Elie Wiesel asked, "Where is God in the camps?" And I say, "Where is God in the Castro?" As a kid I had to go through the Holocaust losing all my relatives in Europe.

And I've stopped speaking at funerals. I have the *mo-ach,* the soul, for it but I don't have the *co-ach,* the strength. I just can't do a speech without crying.

I'm feeling very bitter now. I really don't care about myself at this point. Yeah, I'll take any medications now, but I have my limits. I'm not going to suffer like Frank did. I don't have to go to the last inning.

[T W O   Y E A R S   L A T E R]

I'm feeling good about my AIDS. I'm on the protease inhibitors. Eighteen pills a day. I just got back from a twenty-one-day trip to Paris and New York. Two years ago I couldn't have made the trip. I could barely walk.

I got helped a lot by a wonderful acupuncturist, Misha Cohen. Her practice is called Chicken Soup Chinese Medicine. I go to see her once a week for my neuropathy. Fortunately my insurance covers it. Whatever she does, it works. It might be a placebo effect, but I don't give a shit. It works.

Another exciting thing is that in two weeks the synagogue I helped establish is opening next door. It's going to be a gorgeous landmark building.

I also feel better because I'm not going to funerals all the time. I have lost only two friends in two years. Everybody is holding on through these new medications. The *BAR* [*Bay Area Reporter*] for the first time in eighteen years ran an issue without an obituary.

HIV is in the background now, but for me personally, I have something else wrong. I have hepatitis C, which is also deadly. There is a new medication on the market and I am fighting with my insurance company to get it. The drug doesn't cure it but arrests the disease. There are fifteen side effects associated with it, but it could save my life.

Thirteen of my closest friends who have AIDS have hepatitis C. I got it from IV drug use, when I used speed. Apparently, of all IV drug users, 90 percent have hepatitis C. I'm much more worried about hepatitis C than AIDS.

This past year I was in the hospital for twenty-eight days, ten days in ICU. A botched liver biopsy put me there. But during my lengthy hospital stay, I found I wasn't in any pain. The large amount of morphine they gave me worked. Now I know that when it's my time, I won't suffer. That's a good thing to know.

If something should happen to me, my affairs are in order. I've even paid for my cremation. I'm feeling much more up now. My mind is still as acute as it ever was. I'm still interested in all kinds of things, like the fantastic painting show that I just saw at the Frick and A. S. Byatt's book *Possession* that I am reading. If I can just get that hepatitis C drug, I will be in good shape. Things aren't so bad after all.

[UPDATE]

Bernard Pechter, sixty-three years old, died one year after this last interview.

IF SOMETHING SHOULD HAPPEN TO ME, MY AFFAIRS ARE IN ORDER. I'VE EVEN PAID FOR MY CREMATION. I'M FEELING MUCH MORE UP NOW. MY MIND IS STILL AS ACUTE AS IT EVER WAS. I'M STILL INTERESTED IN ALL KINDS OF THINGS, LIKE THE FANTASTIC PAINTING SHOW THAT I JUST SAW. . . . IF I CAN JUST GET THAT HEPATITIS C DRUG, I WILL BE IN GOOD SHAPE. THINGS AREN'T SO BAD AFTER ALL.

WHITNEY GRANT AND DOROTHY CHAPMAN

Dorothy Chapman
and Whitney Grant

DOROTHY CHAPMAN

I'M WHITNEY'S GRANDMOTHER. Her mother is my youngest daughter. I have four children, nine grandchildren.

In 1989, about the sixteenth or seventeenth of March, I was at work and I got a call from the hospital. They said I had a granddaughter and they were about to put her in foster care because there was nobody there to claim her. You see, my daughter had AIDS and gave birth to this baby and just left her there. I guess my daughter thought the baby was going to die and she didn't want to be around when that happened. So I left work and I went down to the courthouse and got custody of Whitney. I got her at three days old. On March 19 they told me she was HIV positive. She was weighing a pound and a half. So tiny. And to think now she's about 5′7″!

In the hospital they kept saying she was going to die. She wasn't going to live through the night, she wasn't going to live through the weekend. So I told them, "Shut up, let me take her home."

From that time until she was seven, she had to go to the transfusion unit once a month from 8:30 in the morning till about 2:30 for different medications.

My daughter is still alive and has five children, four since Whitney. Thirteen months after Whitney was born, the same daughter had Whitley. They called me to come get her. So today I am taking care of an eleven-year-old and a twelve-year-old. They are sisters. No one is HIV positive except Whitney. I can't understand why they all aren't HIV positive.

Getting back to Whitney twelve years ago, a newborn definitely wasn't part of my plan. I decided to quit my job to take care of her properly. I was a CNA [Certified Nursing Assistant]. She was so sickly. She had to have a breathing and heart monitor on all times of the night and day because she was faint. When Whitney was about two and a half she started preschool, and I knew by then that she was OK.

It's strange about the young African American community. They don't talk about this disease, you know. If they are HIV positive, you'll never know. It's a hush-hush thing. A stigma. Like Whitney's mother, all these years she's in denial. She won't talk about it. That's bad. You need to find somebody you trust enough to talk about it with.

I guess I know a lot of African Americans with HIV because I work at the Center for AIDS Services in Oakland. I'm there every day. Usually, after I get the kids off to school at 8 in the morning I go to work. I leave and pick the kids up at 3:20 from school and take them back to the Center until it's time to go home. They do their homework at the Center. Then we leave anytime between 5 and 7 and we stop at Jack-in-the-Box. I make dinner maybe twice a week.

You have to be open about your HIV to come to the Center. It's is a place for men, women, and children with HIV and AIDS. I'm the director of the day center. We serve two hot meals, breakfast and lunch. They can take showers, have massage, acupuncture, mental health therapy. We take them on outings.

The youngest we have at the Center right now is about three and the oldest is about sixty. Besides African Americans, we have Mexicans, Asians, all kinds of people. The Center is partly funded by Ryan White, and then we get money from the county and private donors. We give three benefits a year, and on Wednesdays we started having bingo to raise money. Some days we see fifty or sixty in the Center, some days a hundred. We give them bus tickets and food vouchers and this kind of stuff. And we have case management and help with housing. A lot of them are alone and just don't have family to be around so they're around the Center. So we try to be a family and make it comfortable for everybody. The Center was started by a gentleman out of Mother Theresa's order. When I first started working there, Mother Theresa came down and visited for a day and that was great.

Most of the people we see got HIV by sex or IV drugs, mostly drugs. A lot of women got it through prostitution. I found out my daughter, Whitney's mother, started out on drugs real early.

Usually I sit at the front desk every day with the sign-in sheet and laundry sheet because they can wash their clothes at the Center. At 9:30 when we open everybody comes in, and most people want towels and soap to shower. There are still a lot of people that are just homeless, that have no place to go. A lot of them sleep in the street. Even if they have families, the families don't want to be bothered because when people are on drugs for so long, it's hard to trust them again in your house. I can understand that.

We get a lot of them in drug meetings, NA meetings twice a week. Some people have been successful, some have relapsed, and some just don't want to go. Like my daughter. They say everybody has a bottom, you'll stop somewhere. But I don't know where the bottom is for her because she's been through an awful lot and she still does the same thing over and over and over, using drugs. Crack cocaine and heroin are the drugs they're using.

And then I just talk to people about what's happening in their lives, their plans. Some say the same thing over and over, but you got to listen. If a client passes, we have a memorial service for them, this type of thing. On the weekend the Center is closed. That's what's so sad. I have a couple that call me every day at home. I hug everybody. That's what they need, a good hug and a good kiss. That's how I know HIV can't be caught just by contact. I'd be in trouble. I say to them, "I love you."

God's in my life every day. I try to treat people like how I like to be treated, regardless of race, creed, whatever. Sometimes I go to church. But to me the church is in your heart. You can't serve God without serving fellow man.

I told you Whitney weighed less than a pound when she was born. I carried her in a shoe box, she was so tiny. This one friend who just died still called her "Shoe Box." I call her my "miracle baby." There is a purpose for her being here. She should find out what that purpose is.

Whitney goes to Camp Sunburst every summer for a week. It's a wonderful camp for kids with HIV and AIDS. A lot of the women haven't told their kids they're HIV, and this is a place where they can come talk about it or find someone to help them tell their kids. It's very heart warming.

The parents go with the kids to camp. It's great. Once the kids get to be twelve, the parents can't go to camp. I am going to protest! But you know, teenagers don't want their parents at camp.

WHITNEY GRANT

I really like going to camp. It's different from school because almost everybody there has HIV or AIDS. At school, my classmates and my teachers don't know I'm HIV positive but the principal does. At camp I get along with everybody great. Sometimes the whole cabin will talk about HIV, or like you and your counselor will talk about it. I meet new people, I hang out with my old friends, the food is good, and we do activities. We have Olympic Day. I like basketball, kickball, baseball. We talk about the virus and about our friends that died. Like last month, one of my friends died. His name was Cory. That was very sad.

IF I HAD THREE WISHES, I'D WISH TO LIVE A BETTER LIFE—NO MORE RACISM, EVERYBODY GETTING ALONG WITH EVERYBODY—TO HAVE MY VIRUS GO AWAY, AND FOR GRANNY TO GET A BIGGER HOUSE.

DOROTHY

The only bad part is when the week ends and you have to leave. Everybody's crying. You're afraid you aren't going to see each other again and that kind of stuff. Most of the time between camps, one of the kids dies, and that brings up issues with the kids. And there's this quilt with the kid's name on it that died. And kids have questions about it. Campfire night they sing songs, very emotional.

WHITNEY

If I had three wishes, I'd wish to live a better life—no more racism, everybody getting along with everybody—to have my virus go away, and for Granny to get a bigger house.

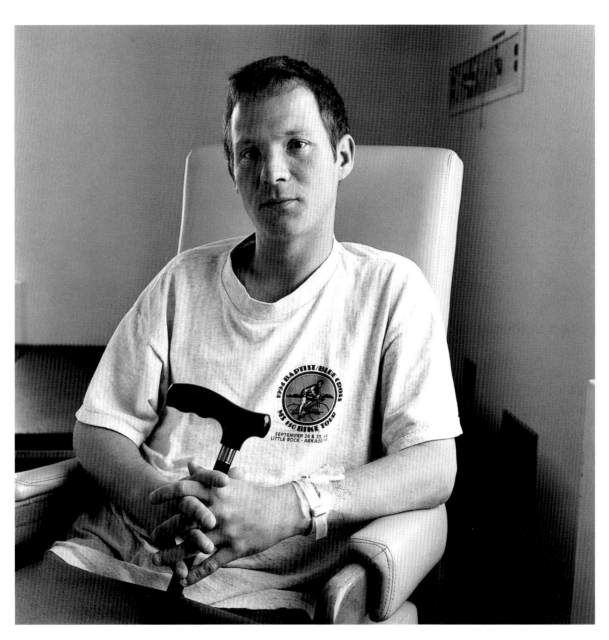

RICCI JO MOIX

Ricci Jo Moix

[IN ST. FRANCIS HOSPITAL, SAN FRANCISCO]

I'M THIRTY-ONE YEARS OLD but I feel like an old man. I'm from Arkansas, the Ozark Mountains. I was a hillbilly growing up. My parents still are. I miss Arkansas right now. I miss being back on the mountain. It's been a year since I've been home.

We were way out in the country, thirty-two miles from the nearest paved road. We were up on the side of the mountain, a community called Skunk Hollar, 502 people. I could probably write down all of their names for you.

I'm second of thirteen children. I went to school about fifty miles from the house, a Catholic school in Conway, a town of about sixteen thousand. My grandmother carried us back and forth until she passed away and then my grandfather started. There were twenty-eight kids in my graduating class and twenty-one of us were related. A Catholic community right in the middle of the Baptist Bible Belt.

Being a hillbilly has to do with how you live. Do you take care of your own? Do you stick together no matter what? That's why feuds last one hundred years and they don't even remember what it was about.

I can remember getting caught when I was about fourteen years old having sex with a boy. Somebody calling my mom. And they used the Q word and all that. She said, "Oh, he's not being queer. Ric's just being Ric." And that's how they looked at it. It wasn't anything strange. It was just being me.

I was first diagnosed with GRID [Gay Related Immune Disorder] in '83. The street name for it was "Gay Cancer." When I found out my diagnosis, my old self died and the medical person came in. Since my diagnosis I've studied this disease. I keep up with Project Inform and read different magazines and books. You learn about medicines as they come out, even before they come out. Sometimes you can even tell your doctor how he can access those medicines for you. I'm fighting for my life and I will try anything.

How do I feel? I just ache all over. I can't point to a spot and say, "I hurt here." And I'm tired all the time. A lot of diarrhea and stuff. My health really sucks. I've got two T cells left and my viral load is a little over a million five, which is not very good at all. I've got non-Hodgkin's lymphoma, and I have in my body a microscopic spore that's in the drinking water. You have to have a severely depressed immune system to get it. It causes you to lose weight. I know I'm still a big guy, but I've lost about thirty-five pounds in three weeks.

I had moved to San Francisco from Little Rock for health care reasons. Me and a friend in Arkansas were listening to a program. There was a story about a leading AIDS practice in San Francisco. I told my friend, "If I can get an appointment with these doctors, I'm leaving tomorrow." So I called the next morning and got an appointment and I jumped on a Greyhound. I didn't know a soul in San Francisco except I had a doctor's appointment and was excited.

When I got off the bus I didn't even know where to go. I've never been homeless in my life until I came to San Francisco. But I ended up doing stuff I thought I would never do. You get so tired you just lay down and sleep on the sidewalk.

I slept in Civic Center Park. The third night I was out on the streets my shoes were stolen while I was sleeping. That's when I realized how rough, how cruel the world could be. Well, it probably wasn't the homeless people that stole from me. But it might have been.

Now that I have been in San Francisco awhile, I feel I have a little community. All the homeless guys with AIDS who go to Shanti to get their breakfast at the Breakfast Club—it's a real strong sense of family there. And I know some Cantonese senior citizens. I drop by their Center and converse.

And then there's Dr. McCuskey. He's my doctor. I call him and just bullshit. Sometimes no health questions at all. And he'll come by and see me and might sit for an hour in the morning and he'll be back tonight and sit for an hour. He might bring me a piece of pie his wife made. He reminds me of my grandfather. He really does. I've told him that. My grandfather, my dad's father, was a kind, wise old man. One of my daddy's brothers made a comment about me, about the homosexual thing. My grandfather laughed and said, "Well, you know, it's a good thing everybody has different taste or everybody would be in love with Grandma." And my grandfather really felt that way because he really loved my grandma.

A lot of the homeless have come up and hung out with me here at St. Francis

IT'S SCARY HOW MANY HOMELESS PEOPLE HAVE AIDS. THE ONES WHO HAVE NOTHING ARE THE ONES WHO WILL GIVE YOU EVERYTHING THEY HAVE. AND THE ONES WHO HAVE EVERYTHING WON'T GIVE YOU NOTHING. . . . I'D BE ON THE STREET AND HOMELESS AND HUNGRY AND CALL AND LIE AND TELL MAMA, "OH, I'M DOING FINE, I'M DOING FINE."

Hospital. They'll buy a pack of cigarettes and bring you eight of them. I take offense when the nurse says, "Where did you meet those friends?"

It's scary how many homeless people have AIDS. The ones who have nothing are the ones who will give you everything they have. And the ones who have everything won't give you nothing.

I would never ask my parents for help. I'd be on the streets and homeless and hungry and call and lie and tell Mama, "Oh, I'm doing fine, I'm doing fine." AIDS has taken a lot away from me, but it hasn't taken my pride. Maybe some of my pride but not all of my dignity. I haven't begged for change on the street and I haven't asked my parents for money.

There's no night I wanted to be on the street. But the shelters are full. You have to play a lottery system to get into them. You go there between six and seven in the morning and pick up a ticket. It looks like those old door prize tickets. At four that afternoon they'll put a list up of the tickets they drew. If they didn't draw your ticket, you didn't get in. At shelters you go to bed at 10 at night and get up at 6 in the morning and you have to be out by 7. And you have nowhere to go at 7.

If I can get well enough, I would like to get out of this hospital and go into low-level supportive living where there is care if you need it but you are basically independent. Gosh, it's such a little thing to worry about, but at this point in my life, it's the only thing I have to work for. Just to get a little bit better.

[THREE WEEKS LATER IN A CHEERY, NEWLY BUILT SUBSIDIZED STUDIO APARTMENT ON PERRY STREET]
This apartment costs $985. And I hate to say it, but being in the hospital two months gave me the chance to save money.

My friends from the street came to see me when I was in the hospital and they come to see me here too. They know I don't have much, but whatever I have they can get. If they are hungry, I will give them some food. They can take a shower. I know I could ask them for anything. They would like a place like this. They would take care of it. All of my homeless friends are glad I have this place even though they are still out there.

So many of them feel like society has wrote 'em off and threw 'em away. But there's a lot of good people out there. You know, there's a big homeless camp right out here under the interstate. Most of them have AIDS. And right here, just in the next block, in the alley, where St. Vincent De Paul is, there are about twenty guys who sleep in the parking lot. You see, they don't have any choice. They have to sleep somewhere. And if they stick together, it's safer than being alone.

A lot of them are strung out on drugs. I think 90 percent of addicts are addicts because they don't know how to cope with reality. A lot of it's lost hope. They feel their families have rejected them. They end up on the streets.

When you first saw me I was about 140 pounds. Well, I'm 165 now. I'm eating everything you aren't supposed to eat to put on weight. I smoke marijuana—medical marijuana, not for recreation. A lot of people say I'm not clean.

I want to live as much as I can. The thought of leaving scares the hell out of me. If I had stayed in Arkansas, I would be dead by now. Had I not got this apartment, Dr. McCuskey was going to put me in the Zen House, which is a hospice. This was like my last grasp at independence, and I was glad to be able to hold on to it. I can't say enough nice things about Dr. McCuskey. He has walked the extra mile. It has really made me feel good.

[SIX MONTHS LATER IN AN APARTMENT ON ROSE STREET]
I'm taking pain medications including morphine. I have nineteen marijuana plants growing in the back. Because my lungs are in such bad shape I can't smoke, so I make a tincture of marijuana, triple sec, and brandy, a quarter cup of each one. You soak ten parts marijuana to one part liquid for ten days and then you drain it. It cures the nauseous part. I'm taking over two hundred pills a day.

Awhile back I saw somebody I knew as an acquaintance at the Food Bank. He looked really bad and he needed someone to take care of him. So I started coming over here to this apartment and taking care of him. When he died, in his will he had listed me as a domestic partner, which guaranteed me the rent control on the apartment, and left me everything—car, house full of furniture. So I left my first little apartment for this one.

Now a have a health care worker named Luis. He has full-blown AIDS but he's doing OK. He has this zest for life. He enjoys helping people. He can do laundry or assist with your meds or whatever, take baths and stuff. Luis is so organized and he gets so aggravated with me sometimes. Actually, what it is, he's a power freak. Like he's handling everything now. I think he thrives on the fact that he has all that author-ity. At this point, this is what I need, somebody to take over, somebody I can trust. I get real dizzy now when I get up, so when I go to the bathroom, day or night, I call him and he comes with me.

Since I last saw you I was clipping dogs at a dog groomer's. I loved going there. When I feel better I can just go there again and hang out and I'm sure I will.

You ask about those homeless people we spoke about last time. All those people that I thought were so helpful when I ended up on the streets, and told me where the food line was and I have invited several of them into my home, to take a shower, to wash their clothes because I have a washer and dryer—just trying to be helpful. Well, stuff has come up missing. I know it was a certain homeless guy who stole an antique watch I had. I had let him come take a shower when I wasn't here. Somebody else stole a checkbook from me and wrote $140 worth of forged checks on my account. I know they are desperate, but it hurts my feelings when people steal from me.

I'm doing a book of photos and stuff for my sister, but she's not going to get it until after I'm dead. I just want someone in the family to really know what I went through. Of all my brothers and sisters and parents, Sarah would be the most understanding.

It's helping me to do it because one of my major battles now is depression. It was my doctor's idea to chronicle it. But who wouldn't be depressed? I'm scared.

I changed some of my will. They had in my living will that I didn't want heroic efforts. Well I do, so I changed it. If I'm dying, that's when I need heroic efforts more than ever. And maximum pain meds. I don't want to hurt. And I have Luis listed as my first agent. It used to be Eric, my friend back in Arkansas since childhood, but I need somebody here who's been in the system and isn't afraid to butt heads with doctors and social workers. And then I have listed my priest back home.

[UPDATE]

Ricci Jo Moix died eighteen months after this last interview. Luis collected money in a cup on Market Street for Ricci's funeral.

SUSAN RODRIGUEZ WITH CHRISTINA,
JOSEPH, AND SAMANTHA

Susan Rodriguez

MORE THAN LIKELY I got infected through my husband, but I don't think that's relevant. My husband was very sick and he got an AIDS diagnosis. So my children and I got tested. Christina, my middle child, tested positive. My older daughter, Samantha, and my youngest child, Joey, are negative. My husband has since died of AIDS.

When I was first diagnosed with HIV in '95, I was not looking to be around anyone who was positive. I was not looking for a support group. I was not looking to cry on anybody's shoulder. I was dealing with a lot of overwhelming stuff. There was no way I was going to sit in a group and start crying.

It was like taking a crash course in this disease because I really knew nothing about it. But I knew in order to save myself and help my daughter I had to educate myself. I saw myself in a hole with no light and I needed something to hold on to. So I would read. There was not a lot of information out there, even in New York City, where I live. I remember going to the library and there was a magazine, *Body Positive.* And I said, "This can't be." There was a whole other world out there and I was going into it.

I am a control freak and I had lost total control in my life. I would ask my doctor questions. I went to the pharmacy in this gay community and just started asking questions. The only component that made sense to me—because there weren't a lot of drugs out there at the time—was nutrition, eating properly.

My daughter was not quite four when she got her diagnosis. Before that she had been sick for a long time, chronically ill after age two. Even though she was developing all these symptoms, like enlarged lymph glands that had to be drained, no flags went up.

She was put in a clinical trial a week after her diagnosis. I got very friendly with the nutritionist who was part of the team and learned a lot from her. I found that my daughter was doing much better once she was eating better and I was eating better.

I had health insurance from the law firm I worked for but she didn't. The clinical trial was my major resource for her to obtain the optimum care. They did neuropsych evaluations, they did MRIs, they did echocardiograms. She got a lot of services.

I used to have disclosure issues. When my middle daughter was in a day care setting I would say to her, "No, don't tell them you had to go to the hospital. Don't show them your arm." I was terrified that somebody would find out. I had moved with my children to my mother's. For eight months I said nothing to my mother about our health situation. It must have been very hard on her.

After some time I was asked to be on the cover of *POZ,* a magazine about HIV and AIDS, so I finally told my mother about my HIV diagnosis. She was very supportive. I told my older daughter—she was eight at the time. She was in severe depression because her father had passed away. She didn't know why he died. Everybody thought it was from smoking. She would see her sister going to the hospital every month. She thought her sister was dying.

When I told her what was going on, it was like a weight had been lifted from her. When you keep secrets, especially from kids, they have a very active imagination. They're going to think the worst. Fortunately there were really great books like *What Is a Virus? My Dad Has HIV*. Four and a half years ago there wasn't a book *My Mom Has HIV,* but maybe there is now. I ended up bringing *What Is a Virus?* into the day care and they did projects from it.

I also said to my older daughter, "Look, who you tell is entirely up to you. You don't have to tell anybody. You can tell everybody." I told her I wasn't going to hide it anymore. I wasn't ashamed anymore.

After I had disclosed to my older daughter, I made her part of the activism that I was doing. I was going to a demonstration in Washington for needle exchange and I brought her with me. And I had done public testimony at the Board of Ed for condom demonstration and AIDS education in the schools. After that an AIDS educator came into her classroom. I learned later that after the presentation, my daughter raises her hand and says, "My mom and my sister have AIDS and Bill Clinton needs to give out clean needles." So it wasn't a select few that she told. She kind of told her class, her teacher, and her educator.

Christina found out about her illness through her older sister, Samantha. We were walking to school one day, I guess she was five and a half or six, and Samantha said, "Mommy, Christina takes those drugs. When is that HIV going to be out of her body?" So that's when Christina said to me, "Yeah, Mommy, when is that HIV going to be out of my blood?" It, like, really took me aback because I never put a name to it. She just knew she had to take these medicines. It's obvious my older daughter was talking to her about it. They are very, very close. They're like best friends. And then my son picked it up and he tells anybody.

I feel lucky that I was able to pull myself out of the hole I was in. I'll tell you when I snapped out of it. Early on after Christina and I were diagnosed, I wasn't taking care of my kids as well as I should have. I mentioned I was living with my mother. My son was still in Pampers. I told my daughter to go change him. She had this hard candy in her mouth. While she was changing my son, my son kicked her and the candy went down her throat. I was half asleep. And then I hear her gasping. She was literally choking. I did the Heimlich on her and I kept doing it and finally the candy came out. "Well," I said to myself, "you better snap the heck out of this. Your daughter almost died because you are lying in the bed." I had been concentrating on the health of one child. And I had three to take care of. That was a turning point for me.

AFTER THE DIAGNOSIS, EVERY WAKING MOMENT IT WAS "I'M HIV POSITIVE, I'M HIV POSITIVE." NOW IT'S NOT WHO I AM. I'M NOT HIV. IT'S A DISEASE THAT I HAVE AND I'M LIVING WITH IT. I DEAL WITH WHATEVER COMES MY WAY ONE STEP AT A TIME.

All my life I had worked, starting at age fourteen. In 1996 I was working as a legal secretary. My husband was in the hospital, my daughter was scheduled to be in the hospital the following day. I couldn't breathe. I would stand in the subway station and think I was going to fall in front of the train. I was having a nervous breakdown, and so I left my job. I couldn't get unemployment, but I got Social Security disability based on depression. I wasn't even looking for it. It just happened. Because I was making good money at my job, I got pretty good benefits. I looked at the cosmos and said, "Maybe this is my way of doing something for my community, doing something for women."

It allowed me to work in the HIV community. About three years ago another woman and I started a program in New York City called SMART University [Sisterhood Mobilized for AIDS/HIV Research and Treatment]. It's a women's treatment education program. It's about empowering women to take control of their lives, to become informed participants in treatment, making decisions, and hopefully to become activists and advocates for themselves and maybe for their community.

We have treatment education classes given by doctors, nurses, activists in the community, legal professionals. The information that we get at these classes is vital. We deal with spirituality. We've had nuns and Buddhists teach. We try to deal with women as a whole, not just the HIV, how to take care of themselves holistically.

When one of the women first came in, she would just sit there, not ask any questions for at least a few sessions. She came to us illiterate. She has gone through a literacy program. She is getting her GED. She's learning how to use the computer. Now she does peer education in her clinic.

My official role is co-coordinator, co-facilitator. My reward is when anybody tells me, "This is a great program and you really helped me." That's all I'm looking for.

I have learned that as caregivers and nurturers, we women tend to not focus on our own health. We sometimes put our own health and our welfare after other people. If we are taking care of someone, we might forget to go for that mammogram. It's a really novel idea to start taking care of ourselves.

I never put my own health first. I had missed two mammogram appointments. I'm not going to beat myself up over it. Last year I was diagnosed with breast cancer. Maybe it could have been detected earlier. When I was going through chemotherapy it was very hard on my kids. I had to go through two surgeries and six months of aggressive chemo and seven weeks of radiation. It was really hard on my son, the physical aspects more than anything. Once I started going through the chemo, three weeks later my hair was coming out. My son started acting out a lot.

He asks me funny things sometimes. "Mommy, why don't I have HIV? Why does Christina have it?" He said, "I must have it." I said, "No, Joey, you've been tested. You may have been exposed to it but you do not have it." I said, "Joey, God works in mysterious ways and you know, thank God, Christina is doing well and thank God you don't have it."

I would say that my kids are the reason I never gave up. It was not even an option. Whatever thoughts I might have had about checking out, my reality was my kids. Even when their father was alive, there wasn't even an option of their being raised by him.

Let me tell you, I am so into myself now, it's sickening! Even my kids say, "Mommy, when are you going to buy *us* clothes?" This summer, when all my treatments were over and I was feeling somewhat human, I started exercising and changing my diet. I stuck the workout tape in the VCR and just started working my ass off.

Challenges now? Cleaning my house. Getting my kids to pick up after themselves. HIV is not a challenge. I'm not happy about having it, obviously. You know, in no way is it a blessing in my life, but it's nothing I can change, so I have to deal with it the best way I can.

You know, I dream about making a career move. I dream about becoming an interior design painter. I was a fine arts major in college and had gone into theater design. I just loved to paint, but I didn't want to be a starving artist. What can I say? I was just into making money. I like paying my bills. I like nice clothes. Computers were coming out. I learned how to do word processing and I made good money. I became a legal secretary and a paralegal. And the artistic stuff didn't happen anymore for me. And I think that's where I want to go now.

I also want to keep my organization alive. This is something that needs to be in place regardless of who is in charge. I just want to set up the mechanisms and let it exist without me. I'd like to have a personal life. I feel like the AIDS community kind of defines who I am, and it's not really who I am. I want to paint. I just want to paint.

After the diagnosis, every waking moment it was "I'm HIV positive, I'm HIV positive." Now it's not who I am. I'm not HIV. It's a disease that I have and I'm living with it. I deal with whatever comes my way one step at a time. And Christina, she's doing great right now.

Michael Naraval

RIGHT NOW I have a very strained relationship with my family. In fact I'm not really speaking to them. Nothing happened—not one thing that caused us not to speak. It just became that way.

My parents, brother, and I emigrated to the United States from the Philippines. I was one and a half when we left. My father had been a physician in the Philippines, but when we came to California he worked as a hospital administrator. My mother worked as a nurse at the same hospital. Even though my parents are Filipino, the culture I identify with most is mainstream upper-middle-class American culture, whatever that means. The area around Palo Alto that I grew up in was pretty homogeneous, Caucasian. Those were mostly my friends.

My family is Catholic, very Catholic. I went to Catholic elementary school, but I convinced my parents that I should probably try public high school. Obviously I wanted to experience life outside a uniform. I denounced my Catholic heritage when I was twenty-five. I had come out to my parents when I was twenty-three, which just sort of confirmed a suspicion they already had. When I refuted my Catholic religion, my mother took that much harder than my coming out to her. She cried when I told her I didn't buy into that dogma anymore, when I refused to go to church. How could I believe in a religion that denounces me as a homosexual?

In Filipino culture it's OK to be gay, as long as it's not in your own family. It's fine if it's the neighbor's kid who's gay. That's sort of the message I got from my family. I knew as early as five that I was attracted to the same sex, even before I knew what attraction was.

I had moved to Los Angeles and lived there from 1995 to '98. When I came back to San Francisco in January of '98, I was diagnosed as HIV positive. I was twenty-seven. I have a suspicion that it was a boyfriend of mine in Los Angeles that infected me. I was pretty careful about practicing safe sex up until I started seeing him, and even for the first several months of being with him. He told me he wasn't positive. We started practicing unsafe sex. Looking back, he probably was positive at that time. But I was equally responsible for not protecting myself so I don't blame him.

When I told my mother I was HIV positive, she and I both agreed that it would probably be a good idea not to tell my father and brother. I don't even know if they know today for sure. I'm assuming that they probably guessed it. Not being able to talk to my family about who I am has really made our relationship difficult. My brother and I were close when we were growing up, but not now.

At the moment I'm feeling good, but it's a daily struggle. I'm taking my meds and keeping a schedule. My health is much improved as of the last blood work I had done. My viral load is practically undetectable, and my T cell count is back up. But earlier this year I got pneumonia, PCP, so my diagnosis went from being HIV positive to full-fledged AIDS. When I got sick with PCP in July, I called my mother to tell her I was

MICHAEL NARAVAL

in the hospital. She seemed fairly concerned but she didn't offer to come visit. I was in there for ten days. After I was released from the hospital, that first month of recovering I was living by myself and it was really hard because I was so sick.

Around the holidays, right around Thanksgiving, I felt a little melancholy. But to be honest I never really turned to my family for any emotional support. It's always been friends who know who I really am. They are my support network.

My plans? Not that I am a morbid person, but lately I've been thinking more about my funeral. I don't dwell on it, but I've made preliminary arrangements, putting money aside for it. I don't want anyone to be burdened with the cost.

I'm also thinking about going back to school, maybe do graduate work in the behavioral sciences. I have a bachelor's degree in sociology. My first job after college was working for a nonprofit, an anti-violence organization. The last job I had was working for a public relations firm. But the side effects of my first meds regimen were severe so I quit and went on disability. Right now I am receiving General Assistance and waiting to find out if I can receive Social Security benefits because of my PCP.

When I was thirty last year I came into a small trust fund my parents had set up a long time ago. And although I'm not really living off it, psychologically it's important to know the money is there. I've been able to scrape by between the General Assistance and the money I saved up from working. If I don't need to spend the trust fund for my living expenses, I probably won't spend it at all and I'll leave it to my nieces and nephews. I just don't feel like it's my money because I didn't work for it myself.

I don't feel like I'm going to die anytime soon. Several months ago, however, when I was so sick, I felt I wanted to die. My body was breaking down. It seemed like everytime I got rid of one thing, another problem came on. It was an awful summer. I don't fear dying. Actually, my best friend, my roommate for several years here and in Los Angeles, committed suicide in 1997. It came as a complete shock. He had AIDS and must have been feeling desperate. It took me a long time to get over his death. Now that I know that I have AIDS, although I'm not suicidal, it's not as far-fetched a notion. I've been pushed almost to the point where death seemed like the best option.

My typical day would be waking up, making myself something to eat, taking my meds. One of the things about my meds is that sleeping eight hours in a row is difficult. I get up a lot to go to the bathroom. So I take naps during the day to make up for whatever sleep I may have lost at night. Sometimes I find myself sort of losing track of what day it is since I'm not working.

I spend a lot of time on the Internet—not in the chat rooms, but I go on a lot of information sites about art, home and garden, decorating, that kind of thing. I'm teaching myself how to reupholster a couch. Random things that I've always been interested in but haven't had the time to learn about. I hardly ever watch television. After September 11 I couldn't watch TV anymore.

DEFINITELY THE SUICIDE OF MY BEST FRIEND SORT OF CHANGED ME A LOT. I DON'T WANT TO SAY THAT I AM TOTALLY SELF-ACTUALIZED AND THAT I KNOW EVERYTHING THERE IS TO KNOW ABOUT MYSELF. IN FACT, AFTER HIS SUICIDE, I REALIZED THERE WAS SO MUCH I DIDN'T KNOW. NOW I'M MORE OPEN TO LEARNING THINGS. AT AGE THIRTY-ONE, I WOULDN'T TRADE ANYTHING FOR THE WISDOM THAT I'VE ACCRUED.

I've never been the kind of person that has to be in a relationship. In fact, if I had to choose, being single seems to suit my lifestyle more. I always tell people I'm not the marrying type. I've had two long-term relationships. The longest was for a year and a half. Everything that a relationship is supposed to give a person, the companionship and the trust and the support, I think I get most of those things from friends. Or I just don't need to rely on anyone for a lot of those things. And then I have guys that I date, to fulfill other physical needs that I may have.

I've experienced a very full life for my age. So it's not like I have any regrets about not doing something. Maybe I would like to go to Europe one more time. I've pretty much traveled over the world, except for South America and Africa. But I'm not dying, excuse the pun, to go to Africa. It's something I feel I can put on the back burner.

Definitely the suicide of my best friend sort of changed me a lot. I don't want to say that I am totally self-actualized and that I know everything there is to know about myself. In fact, after his suicide, I realized there was so much I didn't know. Now I'm more open to learning things. At age thirty-one, I wouldn't trade anything for the wisdom that I've accrued. I'm probably more confident now than I've ever been. I'm happy with the person I am today, so there's really nothing I would change. There have been some really down, tragic moments in my life, but like I said, it's all led up to who I am today.

Sherri Bennette

I'M AN ONLY CHILD, I'm adopted, I'm under five feet tall, and, well, I hate to even mention this, but I'm a genius. I have a photographic memory. I never told anybody. It was how I got straight A's. When I was in high school plays, I used to read the play—it took an hour and a half—and within half an hour I could memorize my whole part.

I'm from Pennsylvania, a country girl. My mom pushed me out of the nest after I graduated from college. I've been in Baltimore since 1982. I met my husband in 1985. We got married in '87. I actually left him in '95. I'm on my third house, second boat, don't even ask me what car. When I first got out of college I started out in retail sales. Then I was an accountant for sixteen years.

Well, I just found out about my HIV status a year ago. Since I don't use drugs—in fact I left my husband because he used drugs—I must have got infected by sexual contact. I haven't been with very many

people. Two weeks after I left my husband I started dating this guy. I dated him for four years, so I know he's how I got infected. When he got flu-like symptoms that never went away—a really bad sore throat and fever, achy bones—he got tested and tested positive. We ended up, of course, breaking up.

I was going to a gynecologist and every six months I was saying, "Test me for everything." Well, unless you specifically say, "Test me for HIV," they don't test you for HIV, which is a crime. I lost thirty-one pounds in eight months. I had shingles. But I looked like a normal person, so they thought my problems were related to stress rather than HIV. That's the scary thing about HIV. There are probably thousands of people walking around with it with absolutely no idea.

A lot of traumatic things have happened in my life, but the past year has been the worst year of my life. My dad beat my mom for ten years, I was raped in college, I had an abortion—all these horrendous things—but it wasn't until I found out I had HIV that I was just not able to cope anymore. It was like the straw that broke the camel's back. I had to finally break down and go to a therapist.

I've told my mom about my HIV status and that was hard. My mom doesn't like me to talk unhappy. So if I call her up and have to cry, she will say, "Call me back tomorrow when you are happy again." It sort of kills me that I can't go to my own mom. And my mom won't tell my dad because he is from the old-fashioned school and he would

SHERRI BENNETTE

think, "Oh, you are a horrible person. You've slept around. And it's your fault." I would get the whole guilt trip. So I don't really have support in my family. Thank God I have girlfriends I can talk to.

Nowadays everybody is caught up in their own lives, so it's hard sometimes. Like every once in a while in the middle of the night you just wake up crying. And you need somebody to talk to.

I like to make a positive out of a negative. I've done some positive things, like my book of poetry. What I'm hoping to do is to become famous through my book and try to help people. The thing that has gotten me through in life is the power of positive thinking. Sort of an inner strength. When I write poetry, it helps me work things out. After it's written I feel—boom!— refreshed, invigorated. I write poems in fifteen or twenty minutes.

The other big stress reliever is that I have a powerboat. I've always loved the water. People say, "Oh, you've been having these money problems. Why don't you sell your boat?" It's like you just don't know what it means to me.

My ex-husband, his family had a place down in southern Maryland. Of course we had a little boat. We joined the Chesapeake Powerboat Association. I became the first female officer. When I left my husband I said to him, "You can have the house. I'll take the boat."

I never knew if I wanted kids. Then when I got into my mid-thirties—maybe it's that hormone thing with your clock ticking—one of the girls in the office had a baby. I was just like, oohh! But my husband was a drug addict. And there was no way I would raise children around drugs. So I told him it's either drugs or me. And he said drugs.

I date men. When I tell them I have HIV, they have a very bad reaction to it. So I try to keep things on a talking level until they get to know me. Relationships now go a lot slower than they normally would have. I told one old boyfriend about having HIV.

MY HUSBAND WAS A DRUG ADDICT. AND THERE WAS NO WAY I WOULD RAISE CHILDREN AROUND DRUGS. SO I TOLD HIM IT'S EITHER DRUGS OR ME. AND HE SAID DRUGS.

He said, "Oh, that's fine. Don't worry." I have not heard from him since. It's like some women who have big boobs. They wonder if men like them for their boobs or not. Well, I don't have to worry about that. I know if I meet somebody it's definitely going to be because they love me and nothing else, because they will have to overlook my HIV.

Being HIV positive is just one of the adjectives that describes me. I still feel the same as I did before, so it hasn't changed the true me. But one thing has changed. I was always trying to find Mr. Right. Men used to be leading me around. Or I used to be chasing around men. It's almost like it's God or goodness leading me down the path, and I am exactly where He wants me. Now I feel like I am an individual who can stand by myself. Now that I've finished my poetry book, *In Search of Prince Charming*, I am not searching for him anymore. That's why God gave me HIV. He thinks I can do bigger and better things and use it as a springboard in a positive direction.

CONNIE AMARATHITHADA

Connie Amarathithada

WHEN I WAS five years old I remember I wanted to put on dresses. I always felt that I was a woman inside. I didn't know what it meant—"woman." But I knew about the clothes that I liked to wear. And the things that I liked to do. The fantasy. But my sister always spanked me when I dressed like a woman.

I always thought I was different. When I was a boy, I always hid my body because it looked feminine. My friends always teased me. When I was a very young boy in Laos, they came to my house and called me "Miss Ted." And I said, "Ssh, don't say anything."

I was born in Laos and spent my first nineteen years there. I was number ten child in the family. My father was a doctor for animals, a veterinarian. My mom left me with my married sister when I was five. My sister and her husband raised me. He was a judge. I don't know a lot of things about my mom and my dad because I didn't live with them.

My family had always told me, "Do this, sit like this, eat like this, you have to have girlfriends, you have to marry. Buddha is going to hurt you if you don't do the right things." And now when I think about it, I cry a lot. Why did they control me? The loneliness, the fear. I almost forgot who I was.

In 1979, when I was nineteen, I left Laos. I lived in the capital city, Vientiane. The Communists were there. I liked the way they did things—just like teamwork. No rich, no poor.

But one day my friend tried to escape. He got arrested and was in jail for four years. After he got out, he said, "Come on, Ted" (I was a boy then). "Let's try to escape." So I decided to leave. I told my family. My sister and my mama cried. They said, "No, don't go now because we need to go together." You see, my family—my mother and father and sisters—were waiting to escape. They planned to sell their house, their jewelry, their property to have money to escape.

AMERICA MADE ME FEEL I COULD DO ANYTHING BECAUSE OF THE FREEDOM. I NEEDED TO FIND OUT WHO I WAS.

But I left first with my friend. From Laos we swam. We came to the big refugee camp. For three months I lived there. And then we traveled to Bangkok, Hong Kong, Japan, and then we went straight to Chicago. I never thought I would survive.

In Chicago I lived with my sister. She had arrived in Chicago two years earlier. I went to high school and I graduated in 1981. That's when my parents came over. America made me feel I could do anything because of the freedom. I needed to find out who I was. I saw that there was life besides my family. So when I was twenty-one my friends took me downtown. I explored the gay clubs and bathhouses. In the clubs men picked me up. This is when I must have got infected with HIV.

But I was confused. I never felt that I fit into gay life. The people in these gay clubs were feminine. And I said, "No, this is not me." I would call my boyfriend "husband." But I never thought I would have to change myself to be a woman.

In Chicago I worked for nine years as a waiter for a big hotel chain. I also worked in a school as a special bilingual aide. When I moved to San Francisco in 1991, I had a good résumé, a lot of references, but I couldn't get a job. I had some money from my profit sharing and stock from the hotel job. I also worked as a prostitute. I lived in the Tenderloin with a transgender friend from Chicago. She dressed me up as a woman. When I dressed up I felt, "Oh, this is me." I thought, "Wow! I look good."

When I first dressed as a woman I thought, OK. I thought, I'll just do it temporarily. I'm still a boy during the daytime. At night I'd put on a wig and makeup and be a woman. Almost a year went by like that. I took hormones. In a few months my hair grew long. But it was confusing to be a woman at night and a man during the day.

My best friend wanted to go to Thailand for a sex change. She already had breast implants, and I admired her. We shared money, we shared love, we cried to each other. We both had HIV. She always made me look pretty. So in 1992 we went to Thailand. When we got there she said, "Connie"—she called me Connie, so after I become a woman I call myself Connie—"Why don't you do your breasts to help you make more money? Men like persons with breasts." The money that I did my breasts is not the money I worked on the street. It was from the stock and profit sharing from my Chicago job. It's clean money, I would say that.

After Thailand I came back to San Francisco with breasts. But I did not feel comfortable with myself. In my heart I felt like a woman but I also felt like a man dressed up as a woman. I still felt like Ted, not Connie. I was worried about how people looked at me.

Between 1992 and 1995 I lost Ted. It was a gradual process. I struggled a lot. But I started using drugs—speed. I abused myself. When I started using drugs I lost friends. I lost my emotion. I lost my self-esteem. I was depressed. This went on for over two years. I thought I was going to die. I cried every day. I didn't see any door open for me. I felt stuck.

When I used to work as a prostitute I said to customers, "Please use a condom." They often said no and offered me more money not to use one. People abuse. They don't care about others. A lot of young men, teenagers that came to me had straight girlfriends. They didn't want to use condoms either.

And then I tried to make contact with my family. They reached out to me. They asked me to get help. I felt good because they cared about me. I even told them I use speed. I told them I have breasts. They say, "What is speed? Why do you use speed?"

Finally I went to see a good friend in the suburbs and stayed for nine days. Then I went into a recovery house. I fought for my spirit. And then I knew I was not going to allow myself to die.

I'm glad I got out of my life in the Tenderloin. What happened to me there was the transition from man to woman, and I didn't know how to live with that. And that's why I abused myself. Both in Laos and here, I was hiding from myself. I lost my dignity, my pride, my spirit, my ego, my strength. Now I have it back.

I found out who I am. I am now the person I am supposed to be. I am clean and sober. I go to substance abuse meetings. I went to transgender groups and met other people like me. I live in this drug-free house with a case manager. I feel I got my life back. I got back my family, my friends.

I can say that even though I have HIV. At first when I found out I had HIV, I didn't even cry. I said, "OK, I can die fast. But I am not going to suffer. I want to die peace-fully." I always accepted death. When I was a kid I cried almost every day, and every night I prayed to Buddha, "Please, take my life away." But I never wanted to kill myself. I thought it was wrong. But I asked Buddha if somebody would kill me or a snake bite me.

Now I don't even feel like dying. Physically I feel strong. My T cell is over 700. My viral load is 4,000. It's almost fourteen years that way. I don't even think about my health issue. I think about how am I going to deal with Connie. Die? No way.

I feel like I am sixteen. I have a lot of strength from being a woman now, through my experiences with family and friends, from having been an addict and a prostitute. I feel I am a little girl learning how to put on makeup and learning how to have a boyfriend.

I still go to the Tenderloin to pass out condoms. Last time I spoke at an open house at the Asian AIDS Project. It was very scary. There were over two hundred people and I had to stand up and say, "I am HIV positive." I knew a lot of the people in the audience. They were dates and customers and transgenders that I knew from when I worked in the Tenderloin.

I want to be independent. Right now I am a full-time student in fashion design. And I want to find love. I want a relationship with somebody I can get along with sexually, emotionally, and mentally. Somebody who will accept me for who I am. I want a masculine, heterosexual man! That's how I want to live life. Cook for my husband, be a good wife. I know I'm not going to have kids, but at least I am going to have somebody.

My family taught me to love people, to be kind, to love yourself. But I never know what it is to love myself. Now I feel I love myself a lot. This is a new feeling.

DEMETRI MOSHOYANNIS

Demetri Moshoyannis

GETTING MY HIV diagnosis at age twenty-three was definitely a big turning point. Before that I think that I was much more of an adolescent. After that point I stopped being a youth. Things that my peers were doing, I felt I couldn't do anymore, like drinking to excess, taking recreational drugs, just being reckless in different kinds of ways. I felt like I needed to grow up and take a lot more responsibility for myself and my actions. I really started to focus on my health and well-being—going to the gym and eating right—all the things that a lot of my peers were not even thinking about.

My father was born and raised in Greece and moved to the United States in his early twenties. He is a musician but worked a lot in the restaurant business. My mother is a teacher and has a Ph.D. Very driven. I was raised on Long Island for the most part. I had a very typical suburban upbringing. I played Little League and was in the Cub Scouts and all of that stuff.

I am out to my parents as gay. I am out to them as HIV positive. Actually it was more difficult for my parents to deal with my being gay than my being HIV positive. I tried to tell them I was gay when I was a senior in high school and they really weren't ready to hear that. Eventually when I was a freshman in college we dealt with it then. They were pretty ignorant of what it meant to be gay. They thought I was making a conscious choice. My mom has done a lot of research into homosexuality and now she honestly believes that it is something that you have a genetic predisposition for. Unfortunately, my father still thinks it's a choice that I am making. So my mother now is very accepting of me and my dad unfortunately isn't.

Greek culture is very much like Italian or Latino. It revolves around a sense of machismo for the men in the society. My father refuses to compromise any of his own values to accept his son being gay. Being HIV positive, however, has been different because my parents see it as, "Oh, my child is sick so we need to help him in any way that we can." They're doing the best they can, giving me access to information and resources. They will send me articles about AIDS from the *New York Times Magazine* or the newsletter of the Gay Men's Health Crisis in New York, which my mom subscribes to.

One of the first things my father said to me when I was coming out as gay was, "You're going to get AIDS and die." Point blank. When I go home to visit on holidays they'll ask me at some point during the trip, "How is your health?" It's kind of a vague, general question like that. I say, "I'm doing fine." I talk to my mother a little bit more in depth around my treatment issues, the fact that right now my doctor has me on steroids because I lost a bunch of weight and I am trying to gain back some of it. If there were something really bad going on with me, then sure, I would tell everybody.

I tested positive in 1994—September 17, 1994. Since then my health has been surprisingly very good. At one point I had some kind of oral infection, my gums were swollen and bleeding and just really painful. The dentist said it was very common for people with HIV infection to have oral complications like that. He put me on an antibiotic and it cleared up pretty quickly. And then I have had my T cells go as low as 291. That was scary. Under 200 you are a person with AIDS. That distinction between a person living with HIV and a person with AIDS, in my mind, is a pretty big one. I don't want to have AIDS.

Once you become a person with AIDS, even if your T cells go back up, you are still a person with AIDS. It just means on a psychological level that your disease is progressing. Having an AIDS diagnosis to me means being one step closer to death. It would really impact everybody else in my life on a psychological level. It would mean the same thing. "Demetri is not doing well. He probably is closer to dying."

I have been on medications almost from the very beginning of my infection. About six months after I tested positive, I entered into a clinical trial. To be a part of a blind study feels a little bit like you're a guinea pig. On a daily basis I try not to think about it too hard.

GETTING MY HIV DIAGNOSIS AT AGE TWENTY-THREE WAS DEFINITELY A BIG TURNING POINT. . . . I FELT LIKE I NEEDED TO GROW UP AND TAKE A LOT MORE RESPONSIBILITY FOR MYSELF AND MY ACTIONS. I REALLY STARTED TO FOCUS ON MY HEALTH AND WELL-BEING—GOING TO THE GYM AND EATING RIGHT—ALL THE THINGS THAT A LOT OF MY PEERS WERE NOT EVEN THINKING ABOUT.

When I was diagnosed I didn't know anybody around my age who was positive. It was very isolating. I was living in Washington, D.C., and when I went to seek out services they said, "Well, we have support groups for HIV positive gay men. Would you like the general group or the group for younger men?" In the "younger group" I was the youngest by five years. This was in 1994. There just weren't many young people who were coming out and saying, "I'm positive."

In Washington there was a great need to bring together HIV positive youth for support, advocacy, and education. In San Francisco, Bay Positives was and still is offering those services. So with a seed grant I started Youth Positive, under the umbrella of Metro Teen, an organization that focused just on prevention. It was a good thing for them and a good thing for me. Youth Positive was pretty successful for a couple of years.

I think there are a lot of young people—teenagers and young adults—who don't know they're positive. Ever since protease inhibitors came into being, HIV testing has not been in the forefront of people's consciousness. That's because there is this idea that AIDS is now a chronic, manageable disease. Young people feel it is not as time-pressing and urgent to know your status. If there are pills out there to keep you alive, most people don't care about knowing their status.

The prevention folks say, "You don't want to become positive because it is a deadly disease." They stress the importance of being tested early.

When you talk to people faced with a life-threatening disease, you learn what it means to live in "fast-forward." Before your HIV diagnosis, you thought you had eighty years to live your life. After the diagnosis you are told you have about ten to twenty years. So you have got to squeeze a lifetime of experience into the next ten to twenty years. There is this sense that I don't have my full life to live anymore. In 1994, when I got my diagnosis—that was before protease inhibitors—everyone was saying ten years. Now, with the protease inhibitors, we don't know how long people can live. Protease inhibitors have their own side effects, and they are fucking up people's bodies, redistributing fat and causing all kinds of other health problems and complications. So on that level, I don't know if I want to live twenty years or longer.

I have never been much of a dreamer. That's actually helped me in some ways because my dreams haven't been dashed. Gay people almost aren't allowed to have the same dreams as straight people. We don't have a cookie cutter dream of the white picket fence, house in the suburbs with 2.5 children, dogs, and sport utility vehicles. Some gay people do have that. But it's not a widespread image in the community.

I guess the things I look forward to are having a long-term partner, which up until this point I have not yet had. And owning property, even if it's something as simple as a condominium. And having dogs and traveling and all that. Those are the things I am trying to accomplish regardless of how long I have to live.

I feel I belong to many communities. I am a strong part of the gay community, actually on a global level. Whether you are from Sweden or Asia, you are having a very similar experience. I'm definitely in the HIV community. I would turn to my friends for help before my family. My friends are an integral part of my support network, the backbone of it.

In Washington, D.C., because I was the director and founder of Youth Positive, I was defined almost exclusively by my career and my HIV status. I didn't want that anymore. So I moved to San Francisco. Here I am not the little HIV youth poster child any more. You get to the point where you want to be treated like everybody else.

There used to be a time when people were much more readily disclosing their HIV status. Now it seems they are tired of being viewed in that small, narrow little box. And so, when you are meeting people to date, it's not maybe the first thing you tell somebody. If it's not a long-term or potential long-term relationship, then you don't really have as much incentive to disclose your status. You want to be judged by other things, like your common interests or your lack of common interests. Whoever said that life was safe and easy?

There are people who are still very adamant about the whole safe sex, using condoms every time, but they are few and far between. The negative men that I know have made this decision to try to seek out only other negative men so they don't have to use condoms. It's really what a good friend of mine has been talking about for years, a sero-separation—negative people staying with negative people, positive people staying with positive people.

Of course that doesn't always happen. Some gay men in the community want to be infected. I think a lot of them feel it's pretty inevitable that they will become positive, so let's just get it over with. It's a big pressure to have that on your mind constantly.

Am I going to seroconvert? If so, when? I don't necessarily agree that they should be going out and trying to become positive. But I understand where it comes from, wanting to relieve that pressure. On some level I felt the same way. I thought that becoming HIV positive was an inevitable part of my being gay. But I didn't think it was going to happen so young. I thought I would be in my thirties or forties when it would happen.

I know when and how I got infected. I was dating a guy. He was very up-front with me that he was HIV positive. For the most part we did have safe sex. But there was one time when we didn't and he didn't use a condom with me. He didn't come inside of me, there wasn't any exchange of fluids. But I do remember, though, that whenever he was excited, there was a lot of pre-cum. And that was really all it took.

I prefer to date HIV positive men. Absolutely. Whenever I do date somebody who is HIV negative, I am very concerned for their health and well-being. I would be devastated if the person I was falling in love with seroconverted because of me. It's a lot easier just to deal with another HIV positive person. And you know, you bond over things like medications. The last three significant partners I have had have all been HIV positive.

I value honesty above all else in a partner. Of course, attraction is important and common interests and all those other things. But honesty is way up there. I have to be able to trust somebody. If I find out that somebody has lied to me, forget it. I have had too many experiences where I have been lied to.

I want to experience love and to know what it is like to have a loving partner. Before I die, when I look back on my life, I want to be able to say, "You know, so and so was the love of my life." And in the best case scenario, that person would still be with me at the time of my death. It would really bother me if, when I was dying, only my family was there. I don't know why that matters to me so much but it does. I would think I had failed in life if I hadn't achieved that love.

Deborah Scheer, mother of Dillon

I WAS HAPPY at my job as a manager in a recreational equipment company, and I felt for the first time in my life that I was on track with my career. But there was a deep longing in me. I wanted to have a baby. Somebody at work knew that. She had just fielded a call from a foster mom who told her that a lot of babies with HIV didn't have homes to go to. Grandparents and other relatives weren't stepping in to take care of the babies. And foster parents weren't bringing home HIV positive babies either.

She told me two incredible stories. One infant was kept in the back bedroom of a home, separated from the rest of the foster family, so that the baby would not get his germs on her children. The other story was about a foster mom who wrapped an HIV positive baby in a sheet of plastic when she had to pick him up. I went off. Totally went off. I started thinking about this. I thought long and hard about it for six months. I needed to follow my heart. So I quit my job and became a foster parent. I went into

Social Services saying, "I want the medically fragile population and specifically infants with HIV."

So for about six years I had a series of medically fragile infants. They would stay with me from six to eight months while they got stronger and their cases went through the court system. Then Dillon came into my life as a foster baby. When I first approached him at Mt. Zion Hospital, there was a placard attached to his isolette. It obscured my view of him. The placard said "USE GLOVES." This sign screamed that this baby could be dangerous so use all protective precautions. In all my years of being a foster parent and dealing with the medically fragile population, I had never seen that sign before. He had been purposefully isolated because of his HIV. When I picked him up I realized that he had never felt the touch of human skin. And this was 1990. By then everybody knew how HIV was transmitted.

Within the first five minutes I knew I could love this kid for the rest of my life. I had fallen in love with him. The moment I saw him I knew he was a bright and exciting little creature. His eyes sparkled. And when he came into my arms it was just like, "I found him!" Because his family situation was not solid enough to care for him, I knew I was going to be raising him.

There was no special training that I needed to care for Dill. No oxygen that he needed, no feeding tubes. Because he had tested positive for HIV antibodies, I brought him to the HIV clinic at Children's Hospital in Oakland. His doctor there did not think Dillon was going to survive his first year. He had problems with his gut; he wasn't able to assimilate food, so he was pretty malnourished. One month after bringing him home, he was started on AZT and began monthly infusions to beef up his immune system. He has been on medications ever since, and we go to a monthly support group at Children's.

Over the last seven years Dillon's been pretty asymptomatic. At two he came down with cellulitis, an infection in his skin. At four he got chicken pox, which is a dreaded

DILLON

disease for kids with HIV. Doctors are real concerned about bacterial infections and meningitis, chicken pox, mumps, measles. I need to know if a child comes into Dill's school with any of those diseases. I need to get a phone call *immediately.* The regular colds and flu our kids handle pretty well.

Last year we moved up to the Russian River from Oakland. We fell into an incredibly supportive community where a lot of the guys have HIV. We spent all summer on the beach together, watching Dill play in the river, talking about viral loads and T cell counts and new medications, especially the protease inhibitors. I learned a lot about adult care and made an assumption that our children were getting that care. At the end of the summer in our monthly support group at Children's, I found out that three of Dillon's friends were not doing well. Their viral loads were climbing and T cells were plummeting. There was no talk of protease inhibitors. When I asked our doctor about them, she said, "I don't have any information about protease inhibitors for children. I have no idea how much to give a kid, how toxic it is, how it mixes with the other meds the children are on. No, it's too risky. I'm not going to prescribe them." I got real scared that our kids didn't have access to these lifesaving drugs. Then I got angry at the system for forgetting our children, and I started calling other parents and activist friends. I said to them, "We need to do something about this before we lose another child."

In September 1996 there were nine drugs that had been approved for adults and three for children. Even though there are ten thousand children across America who have HIV, this is considered too small a population for the drug companies to make a profit. So there were no children's studies or protease inhibitors available for children.

We called together a parent meeting in October. Five or six moms and some pediatric HIV activists came. Geri Brooks, who founded Camp Sunburst, a camp in California for children with HIV, said, "Yes, come meet here. I'll feed you. We will do as much as we can to support you. I want to be in on this." Dr. Art Ammann, one of the first doctors to diagnose pediatric AIDS back in the '80s, came to our first meeting. ACT UP [AIDS Coalition to Unleash Power] Golden Gate also gave us their support and gave us direction.

Dr. Ammann told us of a big FDA drug approval meeting in Washington, coming up in November: "One of you and your kid needs to go and testify." Dillon and I were chosen. Before the meeting, we had sent ahead a packet of six or seven stories, personal stories, to the panel. As I was stumbling up to the podium, shaking, one of the panelists gave Dillon a tiny vial of bubbles. So Dillon was running and dancing and skipping and blowing bubbles. And I read my letter to the panelists. Every time I looked up they were looking right at my eyes, from Dillon to me. And they heard us.

What I learned from a press release the next day was that the panel had given a strong warning to all the drug companies not to come back in front of the FDA for HIV drug approval without preliminary pediatric studies. That was a big step. Then about three months later the FDA came out and opened up the drugs to kids.

Yes, I am an "educator" because nobody else is doing it. The kids don't have a voice, and because of that they are overlooked all the time. There is so much change that needs to happen. At Dillon's various schools I had to do the educating. I'd sit in front of a staff meeting and talk about my son and why he's not dangerous to the other students in the school. Once they understood Dillon's situation, there have been several teachers who go out of their way and make sure they catch his eye and smile and say "Hi." So even though I live in a community with a lot of people who have HIV, when it comes down to children, they forget how HIV can and cannot be transmitted.

From Dill's perspective, he knows he has HIV. I think he understands it's a virus,

AT DILLON'S VARIOUS SCHOOLS I HAD TO DO THE EDUCATING. I'D SIT IN FRONT OF A STAFF MEETING AND TALK ABOUT MY SON AND WHY HE'S NOT DANGEROUS TO THE OTHER STUDENTS IN THE SCHOOL.

though because of his age, I don't know if he knows what a virus is. He knows it's not like a cold or the flu. He knows that he takes medications and IVs and has to eat well to keep his body strong so that it can keep fighting the virus. He has always been around kids who have HIV at his Children's Hospital monthly support group. That has been a mixed bag because as much as we want and need support from each other, it's real hard if someone starts to die or dies. Yeah, we've lost children. It's terrible.

Dillon did a coming out at the end of school last year. We were at the monthly infusion appointment at Children's Hospital and he sat down and wrote a story for the weekly school newsletter: "I HAD AN IV TODAY. THAT'S WHY I WASN'T AT SCHOOL. I NEED SPECIAL MEDICINE BECAUSE I HAVE HIV. YOU CAN'T GET IT FROM ME BY BEING MY FRIEND. I'M GOING TO BE ON TV. I'M A TV STAR."

I was just ready to cover my arms around him if bad stuff came up from it but nothing bad happened. In fact, in the summer kids in our community were coming up to him and saying, "That was really brave, Dillon." And Dillon just said, "Yeah," and kept on going. There were about three different children who reached out to him. That's what I wanted for Dill. For him to have friends. He's very different, and he's got a lot of challenges. To have a kid just look at him builds up his self-esteem.

And when we got back to school the following September, a couple of parents came up to me and said, "How's Dillon doing?" It was nice. I get a lot of support, but Dillon is more isolated because his life is so different from other kids'. It would be really nice for Dillon to be able to talk about his issues.

My relatives live in Los Angeles, and they are an ongoing part of my community. They're all cool and very supportive of having Dillon in the family. Everyone is crazy about him. I think their main worries center around me and about how it might be raising a child and losing him.

I want very much for you to get Dillon's perspective of the virus. As limited as his understanding is, he does know that the virus kills people or can kill people. His birth mother who had HIV died when he was five. He knew her pretty well. Two weeks after she died, Social Services called to say, "There's a baby in the hospital that has HIV that needs a good home right now. Would you consider taking him on?" "Yeah, you know I would." It was the first time I ever thought about raising two kids. I was very happy that my family would include Justin. I introduced Justin to Dillon and said stuff like, "You're going to teach him how to walk and you will be able to feed him." He got excited about being a big brother. But two months later Justin died. Losing a baby like that was the worst thing I have ever gone through. It was awful for Dill too.

My world is pretty insulated. A lot of the people in it are either living with HIV or understand it. And Dillon can easily float wherever I go and be loved. Most of my world centers around providing Dillon with a really good life. That's my main focus, keeping the world safe for Dill. I'm always looking at people, even parents in the school yard, and am kind of curious about what they think about us.

ARTHUR MARTIN

Arthur Martin

I'M A LITTLE apprehensive about this project. The truth is that I feel I'm in the process of reinventing myself. I think I would feel apprehensive about any kind of self-description or portraiture because I'm not really sure who's going to show up.

The Atlanta where I grew up is a small town inside a big city. Eighty or 90 percent of the people who live there come from someplace else, but the rest belong to tight-knit communities, divided up along racial and economic lines, where they know a lot about each other and each other's families and each other's business, and proper appearances count for a lot. We used to spend all our summers on the Georgia coast, where my mother had grown up, with the same families whose kids we went to school with in Atlanta. It was a pretty self-contained world, white and very middle class. Those were the Eisenhower years. When we went downtown, we dressed up. When we flew on an airplane, we wore coats and ties. On Sunday we went to church, then we'd go to my grandparents' for lunch and the maid would serve from the left and pick up from the right when my grandmother rang a little silver bell.

By the end of grade school I knew I was attracted to other boys, and I knew that was the worst, most shameful thing there was. All through high school I tried to change myself. It felt like I was sitting on a time bomb. When it came time to leave for college, I went as far away as my imagination in those days would take me, which was Connecticut. From Atlanta, New England looked like a hotbed of radicalism and deviant social ideas, which is part of why I wanted to go there. But I also wanted to insulate my family from my homosexuality, which I was sure they wouldn't be able to bear. So I got myself safely far away, but I kept wavering between falling in love with men and trying to remake myself as an acceptable heterosexual.

I really only came out after college, when I lived in New York for a few years and had a job in book publishing. I was working among gay people in an enlightened industry in a liberal city where no one much cared who I felt what for. Ultimately, I think the freedom to be who I really was unnerved me. I decided I was dangerously undisciplined and I applied to law school, thinking that would be a sort of boot camp for the mind, to whip my character into shape.

I chose Berkeley for law school on the theory that the three years were going to be so unpleasant and difficult, I might as well go through them in a new and interesting place. My plan was to return to New York as soon as I had my degree, but I ended up loving the Bay Area too much to leave. After graduation I practiced law in San Francisco, in a big firm, a small firm, and finally on my own. I fell in love and built a home with another man, and for a while the direction of my life looked pretty clear.

Back in '84 or '85 when the AIDS epidemic was starting I was HIV negative, but I had many friends and acquaintances who were sick and dying. I used to think I was afraid of pain and afraid of sickness but not afraid of dying. Well, one day reality broke through and I got it that I had been fooling myself, hiding from how scared to death of death I really was. So I picked myself up by the scruff of the neck and marched myself out to buy a book about dying—a real lawyer's reaction—to rub my nose in the subject until I got over the fear. There was nothing remotely merciful in my attitude. I came home with an amazingly sweet, wise book by Stephen Levine called *Meetings at the Edge* and started crying on the first page. The book was a real opening for me. I went to hear Stephen and his wife, Ondrea, speak, did a lot more reading, did some meditating, went to workshops and retreats, and I started becoming a little kinder with myself.

ON THE BEST, MOST AWAKE DAYS NOW I FEEL AS IF I'VE BEEN GIVEN A SECOND CHANCE AT MY LIFE. HIV POPPED MY PRIORITIES INTO FOCUS BY TAKING AWAY THE ILLUSION THAT I HAD ALL THE TIME IN THE WORLD. WHEN YOU KNOW YOUR TIME IS LIMITED, WHAT'S IMPORTANT AND WHAT'S NOT ARE EASIER TO SEE.

Now, I don't think I know anyone who could honestly tell you they were totally unafraid of dying. It feels as if it's hard-wired into the body to want to keep breathing and to fear the unknown. I don't believe we stop existing when we die, but I can still feel fear of something as huge and uncontrollable and unknowable as death. And while experiences I've had since the AIDS epidemic have made me better able to handle physical and emotional pain more consciously and humanely than before, I don't have any illusions about being a wonderful patient. I can get really crabby and whining. Up until now, anyway, when I've felt intensely physically sick, I haven't had much interest in meditating or spirituality at all. And I know that even well-intentioned, good-hearted people, who have done a lot of work on themselves and want to live and die consciously, at the end can still feel frightened and upset that they're not doing it right. There's a temptation among people who are spiritually inclined to believe that if you're loving enough and clear enough, your death will just naturally be serene and beautiful. Some deaths are. But

I think that, while it's a lot better if you're surrounded by love and a lot better if you have some foundation in spiritual practice, nobody is necessarily exempted from a gritty, difficult physical death.

When I got the news that I had HIV in 1990, the things that comforted me most were a couple of meditative exercises that I'd learned from the Levines—those exercises and my lover's braveness and open-heartedness.

Even so, the first few months were pretty nightmarish. I remember going on a business trip to negotiate a complicated agreement with people who had no idea what I was dealing with. I kind of watched myself from outside, behaving normally, functionally as a lawyer, while inside I was feeling sick with fear and despair. After so many years of practice, I'd gotten very good at bottling up and hiding the unacceptable.

Gradually I began telling my friends and family what was going on. Coming out about HIV was much harder for me than coming out about being gay. Whenever I told someone, I'd reexperience part of the distress I felt when I first got the news. It was a while before I felt stable enough to risk telling all the important people in my life. Eventually I went back to Atlanta for what I thought of as the "viewing of the corpse." I dreaded going, but when I got there my family were warm and supportive, and I think the trip ended up being a healing experience for all of us.

In 1996 my blood work started getting seriously worse. The viral load kept shooting up and the T cells kept dropping. By summer I was ready to start getting prepared for what looked like the inevitable. I closed my law office, with both relief and misgivings. Keeping the practice going had become very difficult, but closing it felt like copping out. Part of me still had the attitude that, whatever the question, the answer was the same: try again, try harder this time. And while I wanted to eliminate as much stress in my life as I could, the high-stress profession was a big part of my identity. There was much more grieving involved in giving up the law than I expected, even though I had always felt somewhat out of my element as a lawyer and I had missed doing work that was more personally rewarding.

I was hoping I'd be lucky and have some time in retirement before I got really sick. But then protease inhibitors became available, and for me they worked dramatically against the virus right from the start. My viral load dropped to undetectable, the T cells went back up a little. I had lots of side effects at first, but the cocktail definitely worked.

On the best, most awake days now I feel as if I've been given a second chance at my life. HIV popped my priorities into focus by taking away the illusion that I had all the time in the world. When you know your time is limited, what's important and what's not are easier to see. You realize there isn't going to be time to "fix" yourself before you accept yourself—that you're going to have to love yourself as is or not at all—and that you can't put off loving the people you care about or doing the things that matter to you until some imaginary future time. You really get it that there isn't time to live out anyone else's needs or dreams or values.

So now I have this sense of having to reinvent myself, and instead of preparing to die, I feel like I'm learning to be more alive. I try to pay closer attention. I've improved the way I eat and generally learned to take better care of myself. I've started working out at the gym with a trainer, a really wonderful guy, and gotten my body into better shape than it's ever been in before. I've started writing, which is something I'd always wanted to do.

Back when I first learned I was HIV positive, Ondrea Levine said to me that nothing is too good to be true, and the truth is I've been very fortunate in my experience with HIV. I'm amazed and grateful. I've had good friends, a generous and supportive family, good insurance, lucky timing. I am living in a place where cutting-edge medical treatment is available, and I've had doctors who were generous with information and let me help decide on my own treatments. The results of my blood work now are encouraging, and I hope they'll continue to improve. Things are far from perfect in my life, naturally, and I really don't know what comes next, but I feel better about the future these days than I ever have before.

ROBIN

Robin

I WAS DIAGNOSED with HIV in the fall of '94. I had been married just six months before. My husband and I had been together for seven years before we were married and have been faithful to each other since the day we met. Therefore I know that I was infected years prior to meeting him. I have a good idea that I was infected through sexual contact with a past boyfriend.

The years just prior to my diagnosis were watershed years for me. I had returned to college as an adult student and graduated with honors in the spring of 1993. The following spring I married the man I love. We had a wonderful wedding and I was just so happy. Six months later everything fell apart.

Just before I graduated from college I began having intestinal problems. Eventually I was diagnosed, incorrectly it turned out, with Crohn's disease. I was treated for Crohn's disease over the next couple of years, but a few months after my wedding I began to get sicker—shortness of breath, weakness—

and eventually I came down with pneumonia. I was admitted to the hospital for the pneumonia, but my doctors couldn't figure out what type of pneumonia I had. Nobody thought to test me for HIV because being a white, middle-class woman, I was not considered to be in the risk group.

While hospitalized I came down with shingles, which clued my doctors in to the idea that my immunity was compromised. I was then given the HIV test, and it came back positive. My husband tested negative, thank God. I was more worried about him than anything else. I could not have lived with the idea that I infected him. My condition, however, was very serious. I had also progressed to the condition known as AIDS. The disease had silently damaged my immunity over the years.

It felt like an unseen train had come up from behind and run me down. Here I was trying to better my life and then, bang, I'm in the hospital fighting for my breath, fighting for my life. That's what made it all the harder to accept, that I would learn my fate during the happiest years of my life.

I spent many days lying on the couch contemplating death. It took awhile to recuperate physically and to stop dwelling on morbid thoughts. But I was really determined to survive and move on. I soon started working part-time and eventually was able to work full-time again. Now I'm just a nine-to-five grunt like most everyone else! I just had my sixth-year anniversary at work. My employers have been very supportive and I have excelled at my job.

When I found out I was HIV positive, my husband and I decided to be very open about it and tell our family and friends. I come from a big family, Portuguese on one side and French Canadian and Irish on the other. I am one of six siblings. Our family and friends have been very accepting and supportive. At first my husband's folks thought that it would be best for their son to end the marriage. They didn't say that to me, but I think they said it to him. It's been really hard for them and for my husband. He didn't feel that he could walk away from me, but I think he wanted me to give him that freedom. I couldn't because I was so sick and needed him to be with me. I was kind of hoping he would say, "I'm going on with my life, I can't deal with this in my marriage," to take the burden off myself.

I recently turned forty. I feel fine about the age; in fact, I didn't think I would make it this far. After this birthday, it hit me like a ton of bricks that I really want to have a baby. My husband does not think this is a good idea. His main concern, he says, is my health. He's really worried that my health would decline with a pregnancy. We went to talk to a specialist who is willing to help me get pregnant, and my infectious disease doctor also supports me. My health has very much improved since my diagnosis. I've been very stable. The virus has been reduced to undetectable levels since I've been on triple combination therapy. My husband thinks it's wrong to bring a child into the world, of running the risk of mother-to-child transmission. The fact is that the risk to the baby is as low as 2 percent when the mother is on AZT. I appreciate that many would feel it is wrong to help an HIV positive woman get pregnant. There is however, a growing sense among couples with this disease and their health care providers that this is a quality of life issue. As people are living longer with the disease, they naturally want to be able to have a normal life, including raising children. I've always wanted to be a mother. I love children and I know I would be a wonderful mom.

I would consider adoption, but it's doubtful that we could adopt because of my HIV status. Perhaps we could adopt an HIV positive baby, but I'm afraid that having a very sick child would be too much of a burden for me, given my own illness.

Having this disease makes me feel very isolated. Most people would never suspect someone like me to be HIV positive because I don't fit the image people have in their minds. I have managed to connect with other HIV positive women at the Boston Living Center. You have to be HIV positive to be a member of the Center, where the mem-

I SPENT MANY DAYS LYING ON THE COUCH CONTEMPLATING DEATH. IT TOOK AWHILE TO RECUPERATE PHYSICALLY AND TO STOP DWELLING ON MORBID THOUGHTS. BUT I WAS REALLY DETERMINED TO SURVIVE AND MOVE ON.

bership is mostly gay. It's been hard to connect to people I can relate to. They just started a Ladies Night at the Center. I went there recently for the first time and saw women who looked just like me. I really wanted to talk to them but felt too shy. But I forced myself to go over and greet them. It was weird because they thought I was a volunteer, not a member. It happens all the time when you're a woman. People are just conditioned to expect a certain kind of person. Whenever I visit the Center and go to sign in, the people at the front desk always push the volunteer sign-in sheet in front of me. However, I always insist on signing the member sheet. I want to be recognized for who I am. I think people need to see the other faces of AIDS.

HAVING THIS DISEASE MAKES ME FEEL VERY ISOLATED. MOST PEOPLE WOULD NEVER SUSPECT SOMEONE LIKE ME TO BE HIV POSITIVE BECAUSE I DON'T FIT THE IMAGE PEOPLE HAVE IN THEIR MINDS.

Work is another place where I feel very isolated because of my illness. I work as a legal secretary in a law firm. Only certain top managers in my firm know about my illness. I grappled with having an agency like the Boston AIDS Action Committee come to my firm to help me disclose my status. Instead, my employer decided to have someone come in from the Red Cross to give a general workshop about HIV. Some of the fears expressed by my co-workers during the seminar, like picking up HIV from toilet seats or by casual contact, really freaked me out. I decided I didn't want my co-workers to know, even though I feel badly about keeping this secret. No one I work with seems to have a clue. It's as if AIDS hasn't really touched their lives. Here I am, working with these people every day. I am the face of AIDS but they just don't recognize it.

Sometimes I want people to know about my illness, but not because I want their sympathy. I want them to know I can still function, even though I'm dealing with more than the average person. I don't want people to treat me differently either. Sometimes, though, I wish they did know so they would understand why I've lost weight and have other physical changes.

My health has been good, but there are side effects from the medicines I'm taking, including changes in my appearance. I've been dealing with a disfiguring side effect known as lipodystrophy. That's when you don't metabolize fat as you normally would. They don't know why this happens. Most of the fat from the extremities disappears and there is fat gain mostly in the abdomen, breasts, and neck. I've lost mostly all of the fat in my legs, butt, and face. My face now has a drawn, hollow appearance. The changes have been hard on me emotionally and psychologically. I see a different face when I look in the mirror. It's another loss to deal with, to grieve over.

On the positive side, I have really learned to appreciate everything in a day, to be more aware of my surroundings, of people and my own feelings. This disease makes you more tuned in. I want to become more spiritual. I have just been resistant to it, but I don't know why. I do pray a lot, the traditional prayers I was raised on. I pray every day, for my family, for myself, and even for strangers I pass on the street that look like they could use a prayer. I do grapple with questions like, Is there more than a physical life? Is there anything out there? Where I will go from here?

Going to a six-week Mind/Body seminar at the Deaconess Hospital in Boston was one of the best things I did for myself. Every day I draw on some of the things I learned from the group, whether it's being more mindful or even just taking the time to breathe properly. One of the things that was hard for me to deal with soon after my diagnosis was commuting to work. I was suffering from the "Why me?" syndrome. I would look around at others on the train and think, "Nobody here is HIV positive, only me." Then I realized if I just focused on my breathing and turned away from bad thoughts, I could release those negative feelings.

Besides learning techniques like meditation and breathing, I have learned what it is to be a survivor. We sometimes do readings in our group. Someone once read about how we long-term survivors are like evergreen trees. When leaves on the other trees have turned color and fallen, the evergreen is still there, strong and majestic. When

I did a tai chi exercise this morning, in my mind I was an evergreen. I looked out the window and there was an evergreen swaying in the breeze, the needles were twinkling in the sunlight. I visualize that and it helps me to stay strong.

Sometimes what happens is I don't remember that I'm HIV positive. I'm just going along with my life. I'm working, doing things, being active. Even when I take my medicines, it's a rote thing I do. Sometimes, though, when I go to bed at night, especially when I'm alone, I remember what I'm dealing with. I think to myself, "I can't believe this has happened to me, that I have AIDS." It's almost too hard to believe. Then I remind myself that I'm strong, that I will survive, and I fall asleep.

This picture I drew conveys my own doubts about pregnancy and also the bigger question in the court of public opinion of whether it is ethical for an HIV positive woman to purposefully become pregnant. Physicians willing to help HIV positive couples conceive are few and far between, but there is growing support out there.

BEVERLY HENRY

Beverly Henry

[AT CENTRAL CALIFORNIA WOMEN'S FACILITY]

I'M NOT CONSIDERED a lifer, just a long-termer. I arrived at this prison in 1998. My sentence is fifteen years, 85 percent [she is required to serve 85 percent of her fifteen-year sentence], so I will not leave here until 2009.

I have a long drug history. I was born in Santa Monica, California, fifty-two years ago and grew up in Venice Beach. I am the oldest of eight children. My parents were together fifty-one years. My father worked. My mother didn't. I had a very good foundation to be an African American. I don't recall any days of being hungry. I went to very good schools. I made very good grades, but somewhere around age fourteen or fifteen I decided that some of the people I was watching and being around at my school, I found they were quite interesting, and I wanted to be part of that.

I started hanging out with a group of people that drank. And little did I know that my addiction was probably just waiting. I started drinking, and drinking led to smoking weed, and smoking weed led to dropping barbiturates, and barbiturates led to heroin. I was introduced to a guy who snorted heroin and before I knew it we were snorting heroin together.

Drugs will lead to crime. Had I never used any dope, I would probably be scared to death to commit any kind of crime. But due to needing the drug for your body, you do what it takes to get it. I'm here because I made a $20 sale to an undercover. A lot of the people I knew in high school, most of them that entered a life of crime and drugs, most of them are in prison or out there still using.

There are a lot of drugs in prison. Just like anywhere else, people will try to continue to do things that are illegal. In my case, I have suffered the consequences.

You can get HIV in prison. HIV might even be out of control in prison. People get it through tattooing, unsafe sex, and sharing needles. We are not allowed to tattoo in prison. It's not OK to have sex in prison. It's illegal to do drugs in prison. But some people don't want to change their behavior, and the staff can't be everywhere all the time to check on people. Some of the ink for tattoos was found to have HIV and hepatitis in it.

I came here already diagnosed with HIV. I didn't really know a lot about being HIV positive. What I knew was it affected gay white males. It had nothing to do with me. I'm not a gay white male. I'm black. I'm a heroin user. All I did know was that people were dying. When I first found out about my status, I was walking around, my head was dropped. I just wanted everything to end. A few women that were positive reached out to me because I was very popular in the institution. They kind of took me under their wing and it was like, "You need to read this. You need to learn this."

I prepared in my mind that I'll probably be dead within six months or a year. So of course I gave myself a pity party for about twelve months, and then, when I started not being sick, it was like, "Well, is it possible that I'm not going to die?"

My being self-disclosed in prison is not always OK, even in the prison population. There are some people who, because of lack of knowledge or personal fear or whatever, do not really want to deal with you. I've never experienced somebody actually walking up to me and saying what they may feel about a person who is HIV positive. But then I do know that other women who are positive have experienced that. And I have kind of like intervened and they'll say, "Well, we're not talking about you." And I say, "Well you are talking about me. It does affect me because I'm positive." So the stigma is there.

I make everyone aware of my status. It disturbs me greatly that more people who are positive who live here in the institution do not speak up. What I found out was that if I remain quiet, then it is OK for people to mistreat me. If you come into my room and you're new, I have to tell you I am positive. And if there is anything I can help you with or something you want to know, I will be glad to tell you.

Here I am a peer counselor, and what I do is teach about HIV, AIDS, STDs, hepatitis, and TB. This training was offered in the institution, so I took advantage of it. What the job consists of is reaching out to other people who may or may not be self-disclosed positives. We also visit women who are unable to live in the main prison population because of their illness. Their health is at such a degree that they are unable to move around day to day like I can.

I USED TO THINK, "OH GOD, I'M RUNNING OUT OF TIME." NOW MY THINKING IS TOTALLY DIFFERENT. I REALLY THINK ABOUT MY DAUGHTER. I THINK HOPEFULLY ABOUT HAVING GRANDCHILDREN ONE DAY AND THAT I WILL BE ABLE TO BE A PART OF THEIR LIVES.

With HIV you can live anywhere in this facility. But in 1994 I was placed on a yard and in a unit where there were mostly positives. It was sort of segregated. I thought, "Oh man, I don't want to be in there because I don't want to be like them." I didn't want to have it. But some of the women who had AIDS looked fine. I mean, it was nothing like I pictured. The more I learned, the stronger I got. I said, "I think I can live with this."

Upon parole in 1995 I went into a recovery program, and I think that benefited me more than anything. I met people there who were positive. One of my counselors was positive. So I kinda got into the activist scene and all this training.

I am clean and sober now. This is something I have to do on a daily basis. You learn that you do not have to die addicted, that this is a choice you make. Had I not went into recovery, I would probably still be saying that there's no way I can stop, I will just die with a needle in my arm.

I'm not good at relationships. I picked men that were either abusive or gangsters. The more drugs he had, the better he looked. The uglier he talked, the better he looked. I think I thought it was love. Today I make choices. I make decisions based on how is this going to impact my health. And that's because of HIV.

You know, I have one child who I delivered in prison on a prior term in 1976, and my parents raised that child for me because I was unable to do it, because I was strung out on heroin. I don't know how I managed to have a baby. Since I was fifteen I started in Juvenile Hall, and if I am correct, I believe I have spent in all this time approximately a total of four years free in the real world and the rest of the time in the Department of Corrections.

My mother died in 1999, which really devastated our family because we were pretty close knitted. My daughter will be twenty-five November 11. She is now married. My daughter and I rarely communicate. We became the closest during the time I was in recovery in 1995 and '96. And just when we started to communicate, then I relapsed and I come to prison with this term. So this time I rarely hear from her. I do know that she's married. I managed to get a couple of pictures. But she does not really know me. She doesn't really refer to me as her mother. I think it's very painful for her. Yes, it's painful for me too. I missed a lot of good years. But I was strung out. I used to be in shambles.

What I realize is that I did what I had to do. And the best thing I could have done for my daughter was to ask my mother to take her. I was not raised in the street and I didn't want her in the street. My parents picked her up from prison after she was born. So I'm blessed on the one hand that they took responsibility for her and very guilty on the other. All I can hope is that eventually she will come around. I've explained to her in letters that I am a heroin addict, her father is a heroin addict, her father has been in and out of prison. She knows about my HIV status.

I used to think, "Oh God, I'm running out of time." Now my thinking is totally different. I really think about my daughter. I think hopefully about having grand-children one day and that I will be able to be a part of their lives. As for me and my career, I definitely want to work in activist work. Nothing would thrill me better than to come back here or to any of the prisons—I practically grew up in these places—to come back and help them or have a center where women thirty-five and over can parole, who have nowhere to go, no skills. There are women whose lives are just shattered.

So I intend to be around for quite some time. I believe that whatever my mind does, my body will follow. I don't ignore the fact that I am positive, but I don't dwell on it either. What's a passion for me is to outsmart the HIV. See, I know it's a war. I didn't invite HIV in, but it's here, so we are going to coincide in this body together. I won't put things in my body that are going to aggravate HIV. So HIV and I have a deal. It doesn't even matter to me about a cure. None of that matters because I can have a good life. I can live.

JUDY RICCI

Judy Ricci

[At Central California Women's Facility]

I'VE BEEN HERE for four years. I'm a burglar. I've been an addict since I was thirteen years old. I'm forty now. I'm doing nine years at 80 percent. Like Beverly, if I'm not on drugs, I'm probably the most cowardly person in the world and probably would not have committed any of these crimes. In four years I've never had a verbal reprimand in prison. When I'm in my right frame of mind, I'm an all right person. Addiction is something powerful. I can't even describe what it's like.

I'm very open. I tell everybody about my status. You know, I'm fourteen years HIV positive, twenty-six years hepatitis Type C positive. I've taken my knocks and I've become stronger over time.

It's not something that comes easy. You get a lot of flak and beat yourself up and then you live. You know, ten years ago I never could have told all these women I was HIV positive. Today I'm like, "I'm HIV positive. If you don't like me, don't ask me for my Kool-Aid." But people are cruel here. And they are cruel in the world. Except for in prison we can't leave. Once you know my status, I'm faced with you for the remainder of my time.

There are women here who because they know you're positive will issue you your own spray bottles so you can spray the sink or shower after you use it because of their ideas about HIV transmission. They still think you can get infected if you share a cigarette or drink out of somebody's cup. But telling you my status is not something I owe you if I'm not sleeping with you or I'm not fixing with you or if I'm not strong enough to take the flak that you're going to give me if I tell you I'm positive.

We have people who have died here without ever telling their status. When one woman died, they found all her HIV meds hidden under her bed. So she got sick in silence. That's what a stigma can do to you. I really want to support women who are afraid. I want to help them stand up and feel proud and know they can live a normal life, whatever normal is.

I tested positive for the second time on April 21, 1992. This date will always stand strong in my mind because that's the day I began to deal with my HIV infection in earnest. No more denial. I was back in drug treatment by that time. But I was very embarrassed. I told my mother, who was very supportive. I told some sexual partners that I had because I felt responsible, and I told the people in my recovery program. But you know, I was afraid to have new friendships and have new intimate relationships because I didn't know how to have a healthy relationship in the best of circumstances, much less HIV infected. So for four years I didn't have any relationship.

And when I did have a relationship, I relapsed around it. He was a hobo. Truly a bum. But I couldn't see that because I was so grateful that somebody would be willing to, like, risk their life and be with me. Then I got married to this man. He wasn't the per-

A LOT OF LIVING WITH LIFE-THREATENING ILLNESS IS, WHERE DO YOU WANT TO DIE AT? WHAT DO YOU WANT TO BE REMEMBERED FOR? DO I WANT TO DIE WITH LOVED ONES SURROUNDING ME, OR DO I WANT PEOPLE RIFLING MY POCKETS ON THE STREET CORNER OR IN A DOPE FIEND HOTEL? THOSE ARE THE THINGS I THINK ABOUT.

son to be in my life. Soon I relapsed. As a result of the relapse I went on about a two-year run [of using drugs]. I was arrested a few times, and now I'm doing this time.

I don't know if I'm ever going to be ready, like, to have another sexual relationship, but I'm really learning I'm OK without a relationship and that I'm OK with HIV and I have, like, bumped my head so many times, you know, but I keep getting healthier as I go.

I never took any medication until 1997, when I caught this case [got arrested]. I thought I was going to die here. I thought of it as my death penalty. So I chose to take medication. It immediately started raising my cholesterol although I didn't know it at the time. Your cholesterol is supposed to be like between 150 and 200. Mine was like 485. I am at risk for all kinds of coronary artery disease. And my liver is enlarged. So last year I took a break from medications. The medications did really well for me in terms of HIV, but my liver was crying.

I don't have any children. A lot of time either in correctional facilities or addicted. No time to have kids.

Looking at the future, my imagination is wild. I'm about to do a paralegal course, a correspondence course. I want to come back here and help some of these ladies. I really want to work with advocacy groups that come here. I'm not dying anytime soon, so I might as well make use of my time, you know? That's what gives me passion, really.

During this prison trip I have grown up and I've really started looking around me. I see people's lives are broken and people are really suffering. And the result of our suffering is that we cause suffering on the outside. I just believe in my heart that if you teach people to care about themselves, then they care more about what they do out there. I know I do.

I'm learning to care about myself and how I affect the next person. I just want to pass some of that on. And I try to take steps to make that happen in my life for the future.

I have a seventh-grade education. As a little kid, in third grade, I was in a gifted class. That also meant I was very bored in school. And right out of the sixth grade I was addicted to pills and alcohol and I started shooting dope at the age of thirteen.

My mother had lost custody of me by the time I was fourteen or fifteen. I had been in juvenile probably thirty times before I was fifteen and went to the county jail when I was sixteen under an alias.

I was a molested child, very young. My father died in prison when I was twelve. My mother is a wonderful lady, but I was always lonely. I'm an only child. And so I started using so young, behind the trauma that had happened to me.

I got my GED at twenty-six years old in state prison and of course did nothing with that. But when I got my GED, I passed highest of my class of sixty-five people, even though I hadn't had school in over ten years. So I do have some intelligence and still have something to use.

I can finish my paralegal training in two years. I will get out in 2004. I have two years, eleven months, nine days, and twelve hours left, not that I'm counting!

Because I have to take my medication every day it's a reminder—to care for myself and to teach other people how to care for themselves. So in a whole lot of ways, I hate to say, HIV has been a gift. It has really taught me, or is beginning to teach me, how to prioritize in my life. What's important and what's not. What's garbage and what's not. I don't know if I've been selfish in my life. I've always been very into what I've wanted to do and I really haven't taken time to see what's going on in the world. Everything that was going on in my world has been what's been going on with me. You know what I mean? "Am I addicted at the moment?" "Where's my next fix coming from?" And, "Oh my God, I'm in jail, please take care of me."

I'm really just starting to look around me and think about how can I change some things that aren't working. Just how can I be remembered for something other than being a negative person, an addict, a thief? A lot of living with life-threatening illness is, where do you want to die at? What do you want to be remembered for? Do I want to die with loved ones surrounding me, or do I want people rifling my pockets on the street corner or in a dope fiend hotel? Those are the things I think about. Had I not been arrested, I would probably be dead. Nine years at 80 percent is a little more lesson than I needed. But it has not been all a bad thing. I needed time to sit down in order to get my heart and head together. And it's coming together. I think adversity has a way of waking you up sometimes.

At forty years old I'm just starting to dream of things that I should have had in a normal life. I don't think I ever dreamed of anything but just being safe or not hurt. You know what I mean? Got to stay alive long enough to achieve these new dreams.

RON WILMOT

Ron Wilmot

THE LATE '70s, early '80s were heady times in San Francisco and elsewhere in the world. It was a really exciting time to be alive. We had elected politicians who were openly gay and lesbian. As an openly gay man, I bought a real estate company in 1980 and built it up over time to fifty-two employees. I felt very empowered, very liberated, very legitimate. Those early years were really about work and building my business, building my personal sales. That's where my focus was. I was in my prime energy years. I was working horrific hours—sometimes sixty-five- and seventy-hour weeks to get the business off the ground. But we succeeded. It felt good to be a pioneering gay businessman.

There was a lot of talk going on as early as 1980 about this strange new disease that was affecting gay men. Back then some people were talking about an agent that had been put somewhere in gay bars by the government. This was not so long after the Nixon era, so it was still a very suspicious time. By

1981 the medical establishment had coined a term which they called GLNS, which stood for Gay Lymph Node Syndrome. In later years that categorization became what we now know as HIV disease.

I went in for a routine checkup in late 1980. My lymph nodes were swollen in my groin and neck and under my arms. My oncologist decided I had gay lymph nodes. At first they didn't know it was linked to a virus. They started realizing it was an immune dysfunction.

It was about 1982 when they first realized this was an infectious disease. At first they were saying that 10 percent of the people who became infected would go on to develop symptoms. And that quickly started jumping up to 20 percent, 25 percent, 45 percent. I could see by the progression of the estimated percentages that this was probably not going to stop at 45 percent. I had the presence of mind or the foresight in 1983 to get my affairs in order in terms of a disability policy. Those decisions have certainly served me well, because they have given me a degree of financial independence that I probably wouldn't have otherwise had.

About 1985, when my partners and I had expanded to larger office space, it also became clear that this disease was worsening and accelerating in terms of the numbers of people it was claiming. Yes, I still felt terrific. I started a pretty aggressive aerobic program, I began riding a bicycle. In those days I was riding four or five thousand miles a year. For my fortieth birthday I biked by myself to Los Angeles. My health continued to be OK, though my T cells had been dropping.

My group of close friends all were HIV positive. We used to get together and go down en masse to talk to a research doctor at Stanford, to find out what new developments were coming along. We were looking for answers to prevent the progression. These friends are all dead now. That's been one of the most devastating aspects of this disease: having close, intimate friendships that are cut short. So I'm the only one left out of our little group.

I wonder why I've survived seventeen years with this virus. I think my work is not finished here. I still have some good left to do in this world. It would be easier for me if I knew what that was, but that's actually one of the things that spurs me on, keeps me going. It gives me quite a bit of satisfaction to know that I think I might be doing something right.

Every year, every additional announcement brought it home a little more clearly that this syndrome, disease, whatever you call it, was probably going to affect me in a significant way. This realization really helped me in some ways to prioritize my life. I think many people are confronted with their mortality with a critical disease that doesn't allow them much time. And one of the blessings of this disease is that I've had a long number of years when I've felt terrific, had enough strength and stamina to do everything I wanted to do, but I had the benefit of having to prioritize.

I prioritized friendships, spending less time or no time with the people who weren't important to me. It enabled me to forge a very deep, intimate peer relationship with my parents. It was a long process getting close to my parents. My dad, an insurance salesman, and my mother were devout Episcopalians. So I grew up in a very religious, very Christian household—church, altar boy, sang in the choir. My dad for several of those years had a drinking problem. It wasn't really Ozzie and Harriet. I had a very difficult time in junior high and high school, which I realize in retrospect was just a lot of confusion and trouble about my sexuality. I knew I was different, I didn't know how. I've suppressed so much from that time. I have blanks in memory of seventh and eighth grade.

So when I got out of school, I went to Vietnam with the navy. After serving two of my three years' commitment to the service, I told the navy I was gay. I was coming to realize that I was fundamentally different from most of the people I came in contact

THAT'S BEEN ONE OF THE MOST DEVASTATING ASPECTS OF THIS DISEASE: HAVING CLOSE, INTIMATE FRIEND- SHIPS THAT ARE CUT SHORT. ... I'M THE ONLY ONE LEFT OUT OF OUR LITTLE GROUP. I WONDER WHY I'VE SURVIVED SEVENTEEN YEARS WITH THIS VIRUS. I THINK MY WORK IS NOT FINISHED HERE.

with. I couldn't live the lie anymore, and I couldn't pretend to be what I wasn't. It had become onerous to be on a ship with five thousand men and to be so isolated and so closeted and so afraid all the time. I also thought that telling them might give me a chance to do some good for the gay community, although I wasn't sure who that was yet.

The navy didn't know what to do with me because they had a whole series of procedures in their manuals about what to do if they caught two guys having sex on the ship. But I hadn't had sex with anybody. They didn't know what to do because I was an officer, I had a sterling career. The argument they were using at the time was that gay people were a security risk. My attorney said to them that I would not be a security risk, that I would not be in a position to be blackmailed. I was pulled off the ship pretty immediately. They put me in the psychiatric ward for evaluation. It was really one of the most terrifying couple of hours of my life.

So they processed me for court-martial at Treasure Island near San Francisco. At the proceedings my attorney, whom I had found through my assemblyman, Ron Dellums, brilliantly defended me. I did get an honorable discharge and I got all my VA benefits, which I've never used.

It was during the court-martial waiting period that I told my parents I was gay. They had a very difficult time, my dad in particular. He felt guilty, he felt responsible, he felt he had ruined my life, that he hadn't been present enough. I had come to dread their visits and loathed going back to visit them. On one of their visits I had a dinner party and invited nine of my closest friends and my parents. My dad was nervous about who was going to show up—all of his negative stereotypes about gay men being drag queens or leather men. When he met my friends and saw that I had a group of people whom I cared about and who cared about me, it turned the whole situation around.

Eventually I convinced them to tell some of their friends that I was gay. Well, of course you can predict what happened. They started telling their friends, and there was this outpouring of love and support. So they came out to their friends, to their priest, to the whole world.

My mother told me that when they were on a European vacation, one of the people they became friendly with on the bus told a fag joke. And my father stopped him and said, "Excuse me, Harry, but our son is gay and he is not like that and I don't think that's funny." My father! And so we had forged a relationship based on mutual respect. Although I was born and raised a Christian, Judaism has taken an important place in my life. When I opened my real estate business in 1980, one of my business partners, Rick Cohen, taught me Jewish values, especially *tzadakeh,* charity. Our company had benefits for the homeless, food drives. Later Frank Hyman, who became my lover, brought me to my first Seder. He introduced me to synagogue life and it really struck a chord with me. But I showed up for services about a month after Frank had died, and the president of the temple said, "Well, what are *you* doing here?" This infuriated me. I was going through all this grief stuff, and I thought it was a really callous thing to say.

I went to a synagogue retreat, and there was a big discussion about whether they should say Kaddish [prayer for the dead] for non-Jewish members. And that was a sobering revelation. Those two incidents made me feel like an outsider even though I was active in the synagogue. And so I decided to start the process to convert to Judaism.

What I find so appealing about Judaism is the aspect of praising God in your day-to-day living. That when you give a quarter to a homeless person on the street, you're praising God. When you read for the blind on the radio, you're praising God.

My business partner, Rick Cohen, died the same year that Frank did. They were the two closest people in my life at that time. That was real tough to deal with. I continued to work after that time. It wasn't the same.

My energy and stamina started to flag. My T cells started dropping, but I relentlessly continued to ride my bike because I felt that was the secret to my longevity.

I sold my business in 1994, fourteen years after I opened it. That precipitated for me a skid in my self-esteem that I hadn't experienced since I was twenty years old. An identity crisis. "I'm not president of Hartford Properties anymore. Who am I? What am I?" Luckily I have a very good therapist who really helped me through that.

I started to have trouble absorbing food. My energy level started decreasing, I started feeling lousy—things that made it more difficult to get by on a day-to-day basis.

They don't really understand HIV wasting and why the intestinal tract doesn't absorb nutrients from food the way it should. This nutritional IV is in twelve hours a day, and it's fabulous technology. I have this PICC line in my arm and a catheter that goes into my chest. I hook up usually at 9 P.M. so I'm done at 9 A.M. and it fits in a back-pack. Pretty snazzy. It's been able to increase my weight initially and then stabilize it. And I continue to ride my bike.

Maintaining my health has become my new career. Putting it this way has made the self-esteem stuff better. I am very fortunate not to have financial worries. I'm not wealthy, but I have enough so that I don't have to worry about where the mortgage payment is going to come from or how I'm going to pay the doctors' bills. I tend to be a kind of a thorough guy, so I have three health plans.

What I do with the rest of my time is volunteer work. I have spoken about gay issues on and off for years. Now I have been speaking with Jewish Family and Children's Services through a program, "Putting a Face to AIDS." It's been one of the most inti-mate and rewarding things I've done. I speak to mostly eighth and ninth graders, some adult groups. I'm in my eleventh year of reading for the blind.

One of the most important things I do is to raise money and to show others how to raise money. This year I'm organizing a bike ride, which will be an annual ride to benefit Project Inform. They're thinking of calling it the Ron Wilmot Not Yet Memorial Bike Ride.

One of the things that this disease has done for me is brought me to a place where I am just so grateful to be alive—just a ray of sun on my face when I open the sunroof of my car or a phone call from a friend of mine I haven't talked to in awhile.

And I am involved in a relationship which has been a gift from God. Three years ago at a fundraiser I met this doctor. We clicked immediately. He moved in about a year and a half after we met with his two dogs, which combined with my two dogs. It's really been great and has enhanced my life. There is caring and love in the relationship. I don't think that being gay has so much to do with sex. I think it has much more to do with emotional intimacy and emotional attachment.

I don't have a lot of anxiety around this disease. I really credit Judaism with taking away my fear of death. In Judaism death is such an organic part of life, no less a part of life or less natural than birth or living. And believe me, I have had plenty of time to think about it.

What terrifies me on a real core level is being debilitated and losing my self-sufficiency. It's that loss of independence that I find most worrisome. But I really try not to participate in anticipatory worry, and I'll deal with it when or if it happens. I have a great support network—friends and family and relationships that I treasure—and I think they will serve me well when I need them.

[UPDATE]

Ron Wilmot died shortly after this interview. The annual Ron Wilmot Project Inform Bike Ride takes place each May.

DIANE ADAMS WITH D'YALE

Diane Adams

I THINK IT'S IMPORTANT for the kids who are doing unsafe sex practices to know that there are diseases out there that you can't get rid of. Like HIV. Once you got it, you got it. I got it.

If you look at me, I don't look as if I have it. Here I am looking healthy, feeling healthy. I've had it for fifteen years. But so far God is good and is keeping me healthy.

For me, in my household where I was raised, it was a taboo subject to talk about sex and sex education, period. When I was in school there was very little about condoms and safe sex practices. I mean, I'm pretty sure that there were certain counselors who knew there were certain kids going out there being promiscuous. But there was this big fear in schools, if somebody said anything to this child—"Are you protecting yourself?"—that maybe they could lose their job.

I got infected from heterosexual sex. At age fourteen I got involved with a guy who impressed me with the fact that he had money. I was in the midst of being an emancipated minor and working and doing a lot of things I needed to do. This guy was in his late sixties. This guy's outer appearance said to me if I was to date him or be with him, that there was a likelihood of me being able to get out of poverty. He was the one who infected me. I know that because he was the only one I was having sex with.

Back then I was working for the city of Oakland. It was the summertime. I had this high emotional thing about wanting to experiment with drugs—pot and alcohol and the stuff that I knew at home was not allowed. Most of my friends were drinking or smoking pot. But I also had friends who didn't do drugs and said, "Don't ever get hooked on drugs, it's a terrible thing." This older guy was not my introduction to drugs, not my "gateway" person. I was already experimenting with pot. But I got pregnant by him and I went in for my pregnancy test. I was asked to take an HIV test and I was really offended because I knew I wasn't gay, I wasn't an IV drug user. All of the things that were associated with getting it didn't apply to me. Eventually I agreed to take the test, and that's when I found out I was positive. I was very afraid. But I never mentioned to him that I had the test and it was positive.

I ended up having a miscarriage. All of the things that I heard about people who had HIV/AIDS, that they were going to die within a period of time, really sent me off the deep end. I said, "If I am going to die, I am going to die high." So that's one of the reasons I probably had a miscarriage.

I stayed in that relationship ten years. It was abusive. Sometimes it was OK. I finally got the courage to get out of it. One of the reasons I wanted to leave him was I thought, well, maybe I am not going to die. If I am not going to die, why am I staying with this person who is abusing me? And why I am I continuing to abuse myself by being on drugs?

So I separated from him and ended up sleeping in parks, in alleyways. There were certain times, like during the winter, that I wanted to get off the street. There were a lot of detox programs that I could go into that would get me off the street for a while. Finally I got hooked up with an inpatient program that was at General Hospital. It was forty-two days. I tried to stay clean. But I didn't bring up the issue of me being positive. For me it was too emotionally sensitive. So going into the program really didn't work for me because I didn't deal with the HIV issue at hand.

Once I graduated from the program, I got out and went back into the same abusive relationship and then I ended up relapsing. It wasn't until this older man had a stroke—that was the last straw. He got paralyzed on one side. I figured out that I didn't want to continue to be with him. He left me in a position where I had a place to stay. I had money and stuff like that. But he never did tell me until we finally separated that he had HIV.

I think basically the only person I told about my HIV at the time was my grandmother. At first she didn't believe me. She thought it was something I was saying to her so that she would console me and love me and be kind to me. At that time I really needed help, and there wasn't a lot of help I got from her. She was scared. She was uneducated about how you can catch it. So there was a separation thing, like here's a fork for you and here's a bowl for you and you can't eat out of a real plate. You need to eat out of a plastic plate.

I was raised by my grandmother, my father's mother. My parents weren't around to take care of me. When she got me she was like in her early sixties. For her it was hard for her to raise me after she had raised eleven kids. I felt this sense of resentment for her having to be responsible for me at such an age.

My other grandmother, my mother's mother, reached out to me not too long ago when I got pregnant with my son, D'Yale. The friendship and the love that she gave me when I was pregnant I will never forget. Because while I was pregnant with him I wasn't really ready to give up marijuana and crack. And she would try to help me as much as she could to stay off of it.

IF YOU LOOK AT ME, I DON'T LOOK AS IF I HAVE IT. HERE I AM LOOKING HEALTHY, FEELING HEALTHY. I'VE HAD IT FOR FIFTEEN YEARS. BUT SO FAR GOD IS GOOD AND IS KEEPING ME HEALTHY.

D'Yale came about one night when I was in the midst of going out on a date with a guy I know. He wanted to have sex and I didn't. Eventually he forced himself on me so I ended up being pregnant from that. So I will always know D'Yale was from a date rape. But I also know that there was a different side, what God had in store for me to change.

Before D'Yale was born, I wasn't sure I wanted a baby. But when he was born I thought, OK, maybe I do. I think that having D'Yale is one of the best things I did for myself. Since he's been born a lot of things have changed for me as far as staying clean. You know, I have three years in September of being clean. Before D'Yale I really wasn't interested in being independent and living in my own place. Wanting to have a roof over your children's head gives you a different outlook on what you want to do with your life. I think you want the best for them, so a lot of things start changing.

It feels good to have a child, to have somebody to love. My own family really wasn't there for me. I didn't want them in my life.

I'm really lucky that D'Yale is HIV negative. When I was pregnant, I took AZT. I also was in a study—a pill to prevent the baby from being infected at the time of the birth. The study was a success. I found out last week that the pill I got was not a placebo. It was the real thing.

I want D'Yale to have a good education. He loves going to church, he loves the music. I believe in my heart that there is a separate calling for D'Yale. He does things that normal kids have no clue about. Last week we were reading the Bible before we went to bed. He looked at me and said, "Well, I want you to read such-and-such" I never taught him the Bible verses at all. He knew it word for word.

As for me, right now I'm going to school to try to get my GED. When I'm done, I really want to do carpentry work. And I'm working on getting ready to have another kid. So hopefully it will work out. There are some things that need to take place, like me staying healthy and me taking care of myself. Being here in California where things in medical technology are so advanced, a woman who is HIV positive can definitely have a child that's not positive.

One of the main reasons I would like to have another child is that I would like D'Yale to have a sibling. I think in his situation, with him going to have to deal with me being positive, I think it would be so important for him to have somebody to talk to, to feel that there is a sense of family. The fact that I spoil him rotten—there is going to be a big sense of jealousy if he has a sibling. Hopefully he'll get over it.

I was positive for thirteen years without taking any meds. Now I'm on protease inhibitors because my viral load was going up. If I had a choice, I would go off my meds. The only thing that I really suffer from is severe arthritis.

If something happens to me, I have some people in my life that really care about D'Yale. If something happens to me, he will be OK. Right now I have found a person that's willing to be D'Yale's godfather, which really means a lot to me. This person I believe in my heart and in my soul will be a wonderful role model for my son.

WILLIAM MASON

William Mason

THE AIDS EPIDEMIC is huge and it's right here in Baltimore, the epicenter. It comes out of a huge drug problem. Well, solving the drug problem is going to be difficult. Kind of like trying to put a Band Aid on cancer.

There's a lot of poverty, illiteracy, and social dysfunction here. It involves an enormous struggle just to survive. Social conditions here make substance abuse seem almost like a viable option. So HIV infection is just the end of the real pathology. The ultimate victims in all this pathology are the children. And these children one day will be parents and the cycle starts all over again.

The drugs being used are primarily cocaine and heroin. It's all readily available on the street. I myself used drugs for around twenty years. I'm in almost twelve years of recovery. I started using drugs when I was in the service. That's when my grandmother got sick and died, my uncle had a heart attack, and my mother almost had a nervous breakdown all within a couple of days. I was mad. I was very bitter. A lot of people in my barracks were using drugs. Opium and marijuana were everywhere in Korea.

Before the army I was living in Newark, New Jersey, and I was working in New York, in advertisement, in the mail room. I was doing all right. When I got out of the army and returned to New Jersey, I just started using and it got out of hand. At one point I finally realized that I had to be abstinent from *all* mind- and mood-altering chemicals.

In 1987 I finally got to the Fellowship, Narcotics Anonymous. I was sponsoring some younger guys. They were worried that they might have gotten infected with HIV because some of their friends had acknowledged that they were indeed positive. They asked me if I would go with them to be tested because they were afraid. Now, I had a couple of HIV tests, right, and they all came back negative, and I was coming up on a year. So I went down with them and everybody took the test.

We came back in a couple of weeks for the results and the woman said that she wanted to talk to me. So I thought the woman was going to tell me that one of them was positive. But the woman told me that *my* test came back positive. And of course theirs came back negative. Anyhow, I relapsed. But eventually I just came to the point and said, "Well, if I'm going to die," I said, " I'm not going to die addicted to drugs." As of April 1988 that was the last time I used drugs.

I didn't use unclean needles. I didn't share needles. I didn't understand you could get HIV from the drug paraphernalia, from the water, from cotton, from the bottle tops. That's how I must have contracted HIV.

Now I counsel people with HIV disease. I try to reach the populations that are difficult to reach—the IV drug communities. I do education in the community—churches, institutions, treatment centers, and support groups—to make them aware of what's available medically for them and to try to get them to one of the clinics. I make appropriate referrals if they need more.

I go and hang out in the streets. That's where I get a lot of my ideas. When I go back into the community, it refreshes me. I talk about potential exposure to HIV through drug use and I try to allay some of their fears they have by telling them about confidential, anonymous testing. I let them know that HIV disease is a manageable disease today. For many, yes, this is the first time they are hearing this information.

Actually HIV disease really helped me move away from substance abuse. I have numerous kids—thirteen children and eight grandchildren. Well, I was not going to let my kids see me die of AIDS and on drugs. So I started devoting a lot of time to them, trying to get them on track.

HIV DISEASE REALLY HELPED ME MOVE AWAY FROM SUBSTANCE ABUSE. I HAVE NUMEROUS KIDS—THIRTEEN CHILDREN AND EIGHT GRANDCHILDREN. WELL, I WAS NOT GOING TO LET MY KIDS SEE ME DIE OF AIDS AND ON DRUGS. SO I STARTED DEVOTING A LOT OF TIME TO THEM, TRYING TO GET THEM ON TRACK. MY CHALLENGE NOW IS PARENTING. MY EMPHASIS IS SCHOOL.

My challenge now is parenting. My emphasis is school. "You got to stay in school. You got to do well in school." I am so fearful that one of my kids is going to end up going the route that I went. Anybody can be a mother or a father. But to be a serious parent is a challenge. I don't know if I'm overdoing it or overreacting. I find myself now talking to women and asking them advice. Real challenging, especially when you get a late start.

I talk to my kids about having HIV. When I told my son Robert about it, he responded, "Need some help, Dad? Come get me." And he was the one I thought was going to have a problem knowing my HIV status.

The Fellowship of Narcotics Anonymous is a God-centered program. And they emphasize the need for establishing a relationship with an entity greater than yourself, whatever you choose to call Him. It's allowed me some real peace in the midst of a storm.

People don't really understand how traumatic the recovery process is. They don't understand how prolonged use of mind- and mood-altering chemicals literally alters your brain chemistry. Trying to get all the pieces back together, trying to break this memory feedback loop that develops into a compulsion, trying to break that transit are very difficult. I mean, you have to avoid old friends, places, things. You have to establish a process or routine of new behaviors which in time tend to bring about new thinking. You behave your way into recovery, you don't think your way into recovery. The thinking will follow behavior. At the Fellowship, you start mimicking the people there, go where they go, talking the way they talk.

When I'm not working, I like just being with my kids, being with my family. But I'm never not working. I do my job all the time, even when I am home. People call me from all over the country. People toss my name about freely, and I really don't mind if I can give someone a glimmer of hope. Some people don't have any support whatsoever. Getting an AIDS or HIV diagnosis is a traumatic event, and just talking to people is great. I love my job. You got to love it.

Sometimes I forget I ever used drugs. Recently I bought a house, and now it's not the drugs I'm worrying about, it's the debt! But you know, things turned out well. I was also lucky that protease inhibitors came on. Fortunately I am doing well on them. It's like a miracle, seriously.

I've always been shy. I'm an introvert and I really don't like to be around people. I had to kind of condition myself to talk to a group. I overcame it through prayer. When placed in desperate circumstances, you tend to make some real transformations.

I just asked God to use me, to help me to learn so that I can help alleviate some of the pain in my people. That's the prayer that Solomon prayed. He didn't pray for power or wealth. He just prayed for wisdom so that he could help his people.

Stephanie Selisky

ONE DAY about a year ago I just went to the clinic for a checkup and the nurse practitioner said, "Oh, Stephanie, you take such good care of your body. Do you want an AIDS test?" I said, "Sure." I never thought this HIV test was going to be positive. But in a way I was worrying about it. And when I went in a week later I also got a pregnancy test and I asked her, "Are my AIDS test results in yet?" I saw her looking in my file and her whole face just changed. She said, "There's something wrong. Make an appointment to see me next Friday." She called me early the next morning and said, "Well, your pregnancy test is positive." I was so happy. I wanted this baby. She told me a different doctor was going to give me my AIDS test results on Friday. That's when I really started worrying.

When I went on Friday, my boyfriend and my son, who was eighteen months at the time, were out in the waiting room. When the doctor came in I knew there was something wrong. He's a really funny guy, always has something goofy to say. Well, he came in the room and he was really businesslike. He said, "Well, Stephanie, you recently tested for HIV." He was, like, stalling. "Your test shows you have been exposed to the HIV virus." I didn't exactly know what it meant to be "exposed to the virus" because either you have HIV or you don't. I remember asking him that and he said, "Yeah, you tested positive. You have HIV." I sat there and tried to keep it together. Then I started crying.

The doctors and nurses right away tell you you're probably not going to remember anything they say. Because your mind, your whole body, goes through shock. I remember a social worker coming in to make sure I didn't go home and kill myself. So she went and got Miguel, my boyfriend, and Anthony, my son, from the waiting room. I told Miguel my test came back positive. He gave me a hug. He got tested and his test came back negative.

After that we were just focusing on my pregnancy. We wanted to have the baby. We didn't think about HIV because just to *think* about it was admitting I had it. I ended up having a miscarriage after four months. That was really hard on us.

It took us another year to get pregnant again. When I found out I was pregnant this past May, it was like one of the happiest days of our lives. My baby is due on Valentine's Day. It's not something that me and Miguel just rushed into because we wanted to have a baby. We read brochures, books, *everything*. We know the risks.

Miguel and I live in our own unit in public housing in St. Paul, Minnesota. I have a few friends but not many. My mom is supportive. My dad tries to be. I feel that in one way or another he feels my HIV is his fault. We've never been close. He tries to ask how I'm doing. I'm glad he's in my life. I just wish it didn't have to be under tragic circumstances.

By looking at my viral load, they say I've had HIV about three years but I've only known for about a year. I still haven't felt sick. Since I'm pregnant, I'm only allowed to take AZT and some vitamins. And the AZT is really supposed to help the baby so its chance of being born with HIV is very little.

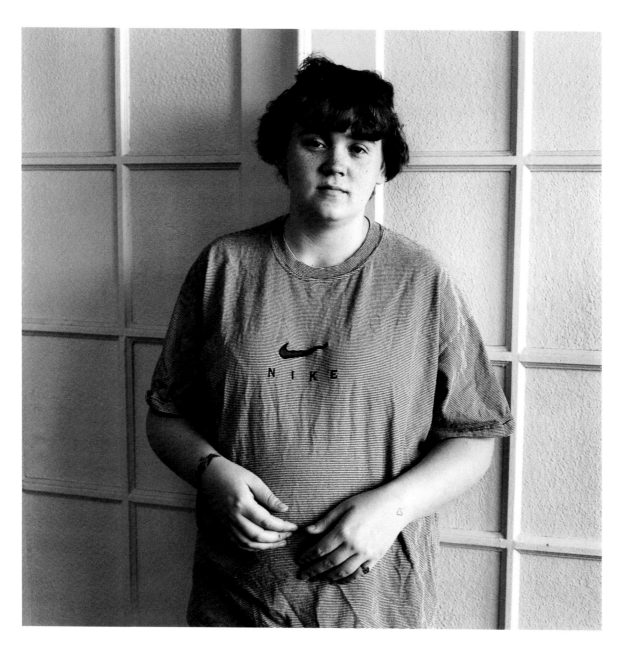

STEPHANIE SELISKY

I go to high schools and tell my story. The first place I did a presentation was the same high school that I went to. And I figured if I could do it there, I could do it anywhere. It was hard, especially because everybody knew me. But I handled it. I had their undivided attention. You know, there were tears. A lot of people came up afterwards. From then on I started doing presentations all the time. It's such a high. I love reaching these kids. I used to be just like them. You know, when I was in school, for sex ed we had the uppity-type people coming, the Red Cross certified, but we never had speakers who were infected by these diseases. I feel maybe if they had talked about it, I'd have listened more and really known that HIV was out there.

THE DOCTORS AND NURSES RIGHT AWAY TELL YOU YOU'RE PROBABLY NOT GOING TO REMEMBER ANYTHING THEY SAY. BECAUSE YOUR MIND, YOUR WHOLE BODY, GOES THROUGH SHOCK. I REMEMBER A SOCIAL WORKER COMING IN TO MAKE SURE I DIDN'T GO HOME AND KILL MYSELF.

I never finished school. I dropped out a little before I became pregnant with my first child. Now I will be going back to school in September. I will finish in one year. My boyfriend, Miguel, can't work. He has asthma really bad. He will probably be the one to watch the kids because I really need to go to school. So he's in the process of getting Social Security for himself. Miguel and I've been together since my son was nine and a half months.

You go through every emotion possible with HIV. First is a sadness. You feel like your life is over, you're going to die right away. And denial slips right in there with it. "Well, I'm not going to die." Then comes the anger. You're angry at everybody who is not there for you now. You're angry at yourself for being vulnerable at some point in time and getting this disease. You're angry at the doctors. You're always yelling, "God!" God gets blamed for so many things, you know, and really He didn't have anything to do with it. Eventually your anger just goes down once again to acceptance and you deal with it. I've been through that and anger comes by now and then but it just makes me feel sorry for the person I got this disease from, that is, my son's father.

I came up with this theory that everything happens for a reason, that we're all here for a purpose. From the moment that we're all born, God receives this file on us no matter who you are. The files are all different sizes. Skinny, thick. It's got in it everything you're going to do in your life. Sort of written like a play. So God put it down that I have this disease for a reason, to learn from it and make my life better from it. Since my diagnosis, my life is better, more focused. It's just like I woke up. Before I got infected, I needed a healthy environment, a family, a home. I didn't have them. Now I have them.

Before I found out I had HIV, I was talking to God one night and I was saying, "Oh, I am just so ordinary. I'm just like everybody else." I was just feeling sorry for myself. "Why can't You make me different?" I meant like a movie star, a singer, a model. Later when I tested positive for HIV, I remembered what I had asked God for. "God, *I didn't mean this!* I didn't mean HIV!" And that's what I got. It has made me become a completely different person, a better person. Yeah, I'm still Stephanie Selisky but I'm not Stephanie Selisky the mother on welfare. I'm Stephanie Selisky the HIV and AIDS educator, the speaker, the advocate. That's who I am now.

I was dreading the day when I was going to have to sit my son down and tell him, "Anthony, Mommy is going to die because of this." We talk openly about HIV in front of him. And I take him to my presentations. I'm sure when he gets older, if he has questions, he'll ask me. I figure by the time he's in school, a lot more people will be aware of HIV. Already they're starting to give sex ed at a younger age than they used to. That really makes me feel good.

I want to be remembered for something other than I just have HIV. I don't want a tiny obituary, "Died tragically from AIDS." I want "founder of this," "supporter of this." I'm proud that I have HIV. Not that it's a good thing and I'm telling people to go get it. But I'm proud of who I am and who HIV helped me to discover.

Depression also comes hand in hand with HIV. There have been many times when

I'm watching myself play and laugh and my eyes just well up with tears. Because one day I'm not going to see myself play and laugh. Who knows if I'll see my son graduate? I would really like to see him go to his prom, to graduate high school. I want to see him grow up and have his first girlfriend. I really want to be there for him.

When Miguel tested negative, he could have left me but he didn't. He stayed with me and we're still together. When I want to really talk about my HIV, he doesn't want to. He's like in denial in his own little way. But he's proud of me for all that I do for HIV, my talks in schools. He's starting to do presentations as the "affected" rather than "infected." And he likes the way he feels when he does that.

We don't base our life around HIV. It just mingles in with us. We just don't think about it because who knows how much time we have together? And if we waste time worrying, we wouldn't be happy.

Ruben Alicea

MY FATHER WAS in and out of my life growing up and he would just come once a month to visit. When I saw him six months ago I decided to tell him I was HIV positive. He didn't take that well at all. He made me feel really, really bad. We don't have a good relationship.

My father is from Puerto Rico. He's really, really strict. He doesn't know I am gay. He thinks I am HIV positive from having sex with women. He doesn't even call me to find out how I'm doing. The rest of my family is my sister and her two kids and my mom.

I told my mom I was gay when I was fourteen. I told her I was HIV positive the day I found out. I was seventeen. My mother's a great support—unconditional, and she loves me to death. She is not going to stop loving me. She was born here, so she is very much more open-minded than my father.

The group of gay men that I met when I was thirteen were much older than me, twenty-four or twenty-five. They were all Latin men. One black. A majority of those people turned out to be sick. Now I look back and I think they showed me the horrible part of the gay life. I don't want to put blame on anyone, but I think they led me in very negative ways. At fifteen they snuck me into my first gay club. And then I ended up dropping out of school because I was partying all the time.

Even though I knew what I was doing—drugs, unprotected sex, all the bad stuff—I just wasn't thinking I would get HIV even though HIV was around me. The day I got tested I was at the clinic to see the doctor. "Do you want to get tested for HIV?" I said, "OK." A month later—the doctor had gone on vacation—they told me I was HIV positive. I called my mom and told her she needed to come home. My mom just started screaming. She didn't want me to die. It was horrible. You know, honestly, I can't tell you what happened the next day. I blocked it out. I wish I could forget about the day I found out, not the day after.

So I just hung out more, more partying, more self-destructive behavior. I did coke and weed and alcohol. I wasn't doing Ecstasy or stuff like that. It's just that I kept getting into bad relationships and I was suffering from depression. There were times I wouldn't leave my bed, couldn't go out of the house.

I don't want this disease to run my life. All the self-pity. It's time to make my life better. Being angry and pissed is negativity. I have a lot of anger. But I just try to push it aside.

Physically I feel OK. My blood work has been fine. My viral load went up a little bit but not much. I'm stuck between taking HIV drugs or not. If you start taking them, you have to start worrying about kidney and liver. But if you don't take them, you have to worry about HIV. My doctor said I don't need them at this point.

My best friend, Jackie, died not so long ago, in June. She was so young. Nineteen. I never got the full story. She seemed fine. She just got back her blood work. Her T

RUBEN ALICEA

cells were high, her viral loads were low. And two days later she died. I was torturing myself a lot after she died, thinking I was going to die. I get really scared.

Now when I get scared, I talk to my social worker. There are just certain things I can tell certain people. I can call my mom but I can't tell her things that are going on in my personal life or about feeling sick because she worries too much.

When I meet people I never really know if they are positive or negative. A lot of positive people won't tell you they're positive. It kind of sucks because when you stop dating, if you find out they're positive, you can't help feel guilty that you had something had to do with it. I was going with someone for about a year and we broke up. Well, he just found out that he is positive. I can't help but wonder if he was HIV positive to begin with. But he says I left him like that. It makes me feel bad. But I didn't put a gun to his head. He's a man. He knows what he is doing.

Honesty is the most important thing in a relationship. I have been screwed so many times. I recently ended a relationship. It opened up my eyes so much. In a lot of ways it was like looking in a mirror. My ex-lover had all my faults. Very unmotivated, dwelled a lot on what's going wrong and beat himself up a lot. And I said "No, I don't want this." I want to be with someone who makes me laugh.

Now I can say it's a transition time. I am a full-time college student, first year. I like my communications class, how to make speeches. That's the only class I really enjoy. I'm feeling more positive in my life than I've ever felt before.

My neighborhood in Brooklyn is horrible, disgusting. Drugs all over the place. I got mugged twice. Sometimes you hear gunshots. DAS [Division of AIDS Services] pays my whole rent. And then they give me $140 every two weeks. Plus I have to pay light, gas, phone. It's extremely hard to live on this. I'm surprised that I make it. And I have financial aid for school and I will take out loans. It's killing me now because I have to raise another $68 for my train fare for the month. My mother helps me out when she can. I don't like to ask her for too much. I want her to see that I'm doing OK.

Sometimes I feel like I am running out of time. Rushing, just rushing, because you think you might die. Anybody can die anytime, but I have a greater chance. Sometimes I rush for someone to love me because I want to feel that love, I want to have that relationship. And then I realize I don't want this.

I want to be doing something I will enjoy for work. Hopefully making some good money. I'm not saying I want millions of dollars. No, I just want to be OK—that nothing is going to happen to me, that my rent is paid, that I am going to be happy. And hopefully to live ten more years.

I do believe in God. God is good. But then I try to understand why there is so much bad around, so much evil, you know. I pray, but sometimes I feel like a hypocrite because I usually pray when I am in need. I'm asking Him to help, yet I don't really do anything for Him. I don't really go to church. I don't live an unsinful life.

I could use a vacation. I have never been on a vacation. I just want to be somewhere new and different and be able to clear my head and enjoy myself. Not that I want to run away from my problems. I just want a break from them. I would love to go to Florida or California or Puerto Rico. It's too cold here in New York.

BETH HASTIE

Beth Hastie

WHEN I WAS a student at Harvard, I had done a research project on women and HIV. My major was English, but the paper was part of a Women's Studies project. At the time I did the project, it did not occur to me that I would become HIV positive myself.

I got infected from a date rape while I was a student. I got sick a few weeks afterwards with severe flu–like symptoms. I went to the university health services. I was given a lot of tests to find out what was wrong, but they didn't find anything, so I was sent on my way and treated like a hypochondriac.

Finally I got tested in '92, four or five months after graduating, and tested positive. This was really, really devastating. At the time I was out as a bisexual even though I had only been with men. I was just actually starting to date women. So I went through a lot of trauma and depression and didn't date anyone for a couple of years. That was really difficult in terms of development of my sexuality. Now I am out as a lesbian. I've been in a five-year relationship with a woman which has gone great. She is not HIV positive.

When I was first diagnosed, there were very few medications. I didn't have any health insurance. Back then in '92 many employers had preexisting condition clauses for health insurance. I had friends who graduated with me who as a prerequisite for their jobs had to have an HIV test, so I was really scared. Harvard at that time didn't have any preexisting conditions clause, so that was a safe place to work. Before I was tested I had been working part-time at Harvard. So I got a different job at Harvard that came with health insurance. I stayed there for eight years.

Once I found out I was positive, I just had to get away from AIDS activism because it was too close to home. So I got really involved with the feminist community in Boston, did a lot of abortion rights and welfare reform, and then eventually got involved in the lesbian community. And then I gradually joined everything and helped found the Lesbian AIDS Project of Massachusetts, which is a grass-roots organization that was inspired by the Lesbian AIDS Project in New York. So finally I was able to come back and be all of myself as a woman, a lesbian, dealing with HIV, and do that all together. And that's been really exciting. At the Lesbian AIDS Project we just finished compiling a health resource guide for lesbian, bisexual, and transgender women, those dealing with HIV and those who aren't.

The primary ways that women get HIV is through sex with men and injection drug use, sharing needles. There are a small number of women who have been infected by their women partners.

Lesbian women with HIV have really been invisible. There's not a whole lot of research because the Centers for Disease Control use the categories of men who have sex with men, bisexual men, injection drug users, and heterosexual sex. They don't track women who have sex with women because the sexual transmission [of HIV between women] is very low risk. Our lives are complicated. The fact that one is a lesbian doesn't mean that she has never slept with men. It doesn't mean that she doesn't use drugs.

There is a study going on right now looking at injection-drug-using women who have sex with women. They actually are at higher risk than injection-drug-using straight women. It may be a combination of poverty, homophobia, discrimination, and social factors that places these women at higher risk.

There's another thing. When young lesbians like myself are struggling with coming out, you may be having sex with queer men. The man that infected me—I think he was bisexual—he might have even been a sex worker. He could have also been an IV drug user. I didn't know him very well. I met him in a gay male club. While I was being raped, in my dorm room, I had tried to negotiate safer sex with him and wasn't able to in that situation.

Anyone anywhere can be isolated and afraid, because the stigma of having HIV still exists. For me, actually, the stigma of rape is worse than HIV. It takes a lot not to blame yourself when you're raped. It was the most difficult thing to talk about. I've only recently become comfortable writing and talking about it. I think it's important to speak out.

I GOT INFECTED FROM A DATE RAPE WHILE I WAS A STUDENT. I GOT SICK A FEW WEEKS AFTERWARDS WITH SEVERE FLU-LIKE SYMPTOMS. I WENT TO THE UNIVERSITY HEALTH SERVICES. I WAS GIVEN A LOT OF TESTS TO FIND OUT WHAT WAS WRONG, BUT THEY DIDN'T FIND ANYTHING, SO I WAS SENT ON MY WAY AND TREATED LIKE A HYPOCHONDRIAC.

It took me going to national conferences on women with HIV to meet other positive women. The first time I met a lot of positive women was in '95, when I went down to Washington, D.C., for the conference on women and HIV.

I am working full-time now at the Boston Living Center. It's a peer-led community center for people living with HIV. A lot of what I do is to make the Center a welcoming place for women. I organize social events and educational programming and oversee a respite child care program for the women's kids while the mothers are at the Center.

About two thirds of the people we see are women of color, primarily African American and then Latina. There are a number of white women. Even though we may have our differences in terms of race, class, life experience, I see that so many HIV positive women have experienced rape, incest, sexual abuse of some kind in their lives. It's really horrifying.

ANYONE ANYWHERE CAN BE ISOLATED AND AFRAID, BECAUSE THE STIGMA OF HAVING HIV STILL EXISTS. FOR ME, ACTUALLY, THE STIGMA OF RAPE IS WORSE THAN HIV. IT TAKES A LOT NOT TO BLAME YOURSELF WHEN YOU'RE RAPED.

Boston is one of the best places to be in terms of resources if you are HIV positive—medical research, access, knowledgeable doctors, nurses, and other health care professionals. Much of the social services structure in Massachusetts comes out of its being a very Democratic and liberal state. Rural areas outside of Boston can be more of a problem, where people are more isolated.

People who don't tell others about their HIV status are isolated and alone. This causes a lot of pain, and it's not always necessary. Sometimes people think the worst of how other people are going to respond. I know a lot of people who haven't told their best friends and they are silently suffering for years. It takes a toll. My partner is totally supportive, and that makes me feel better.

I grew up in Boston. My parents are definitely sort of eccentric. They are both civil rights activists. My mom's a social worker and my dad's a minister, Episcopal, very progressive. So I haven't fallen far from the tree in terms of, like, feeling optimistic about changing the world when things are going wrong and being able to make a difference and also being connected to the community. I'm lucky that my general personality that I was born with sees that the glass is half full.

I'm a very busy woman and I'm happiest when I feel engaged and productive. Sometimes I have this feeling that things won't get done unless I do them myself. It's a struggle. HIV positive women who are outspoken and involved in the community, we tend to get really burned out because everyone wants us to do stuff and we feel there are issues that really need a spotlight on them. And sometimes it really gets exhausting. Which is why we have to help empower our sisters to also be doing that work so that we don't get burned out.

A year ago I turned thirty and it was actually a big milestone for me because I never thought I would reach thirty. So on this birthday I said, "Oh, I'm still here. I'm going to have to move on with my life." I've been able to realize I do have a future. I just went back to school which is very exciting, part-time, at BU [Boston University]. I'm getting a master's in public health. It took me a long time to go back to school because I kept waiting to get sick and thought I wouldn't get through the program or be around to use the degree. Seeing my partner go back to school at age thirty-nine, becoming a nurse, which she always dreamed of doing, was inspirational for me.

My relationship is very exciting. We're at the point where we are thinking of moving in together. A couple of years ago I never imagined that I might be in a position to buy a house or to go back to graduate school or just to be here now.

My health is good. Had some problems with side effects a couple of years ago—liver and other problems. I switched my regimen and got much better. The main problem I have now is lipodystrophy, a fat redistribution. I don't like the way my body looks. A lot of my life I have been overweight, but I until recently I have had a very positive body image. Down the road lipodystrophy may be a problem because it could be linked to heart disease. We don't know what the side effects of these medications are long term and we are starting to find out.

On a lighter note, I play center on a women's flag football team. It's the Jamaica Plain Women's Flag Football League, and we may win the championships this weekend!

MARVIN WELLS

Marvin Wells

PUT IT THIS WAY: I'm poor. I'm black. I'm gay. I'm HIV. I'm left-handed. I grew up in Baltimore. My parents are from the South. They moved up, maybe, when they were in their twenties. I have six brothers and a sister. Everybody's basically in the Baltimore area. We bicker just like regular families.

I got married two years after I graduated high school. My wife was twenty-one and I was twenty. I just dropped out of college and got married, went into the air force, and had a son. When we were married, my wife, it seemed like she wanted to do the same thing like my mother did, just get pregnant and have a baby. She didn't want to go anywhere, have any fun or anything. So I was in town every night, partying. The gay people danced and had fun and laughed and stuff. That is how the gay thing got started. And years of that, hey, here I am. I've been divorced for many years. Now I'm on disability.

When I found out I had HIV it was February 22, 1991. The way I found out was I had gotten into a fight with a male friend—guess we were lovers or whatever—and I had been arrested. But I had injured him, so he was tested and he tested positive. So I got a visit from the Health Department. Then I got tested.

After I got the news I just went on a drinking, drugging binge for maybe about a year. I was self-destructive until I finally just, I guess, collapsed. I tried one of those suicide things, chased a handful of pills with alcohol, hospitalized for about a month, and then I started going into treatment centers, like the VA. Started bringing myself back together. I've been working on it for nine years now. I'm still having a little problem with it.

At that time in the early '90s people when they found out they had HIV, they were killing themselves. They were dying horrible deaths, wasting and looking really awful. I could look at people and look at their fingernails. "Oh, black fingernails. They have HIV."

My disability is not so much the HIV but it's the depression that's giving me a big problem. I'm taking antidepressants. I'm on blood pressure medication. I'm on my three antivirals. I'm on vitamins also. I see a psychologist.

I really hate to say it, but my typical day, it's nothing. It feels as though I constantly worry. OK, my father's really ill. I have an ex-wife from hell. And taking care of yourself is a full-time job. You know, really, I can be paranoid. Like the slightest little cough or something, I might just get on the phone to the doctors. I also have herpes, the genital kind, that comes when you're stressed out.

This weekend was particularly hard for me. OK. I live off of $800 a month from Social Security. Friday a friend of mine wanted me to go to the clubs with him. I just can't afford to jump up and go to the clubs. He begged. I had paid my rent, my phone, my cable bill, got some food. I even had my hair done. So I said no. And he got mad. Usually I hear from him every day, but I haven't heard from him since Friday.

My son is more or less out of the picture. About six months ago he called me at

2 A.M. and he was saying I wasn't there for him. He didn't mention anything about the gay stuff, but I'm sure he knows. I feel guilty about going the homosexual route.

He knows I have HIV. At one point, maybe a year ago, he said it's best for us not to be close to each other because people are going to think his mother has HIV. That kind of hurt my feelings, but I've talked on the phone with him since. I'm scared of getting my feelings hurt.

My son will be twenty-one this year. He lives with my ex. Yeah, he's angry. He's angry at his mother. He's angry at me. He was going to school, a community college. And all of a sudden he just quit. If it's just money, why doesn't he say he needs money and I would see what I could do.

I'd like him to grow up and be a loving and caring person. It doesn't matter to me if he's a doctor or an office worker. I just want him to be the type of person that I think counts in life, a person who cares for other people. That's all I ask.

There are some people I can count on, like the manager of my building. I do the landscaping for my apartment building. "You can have free air conditioning, just cut the grass." Sometimes at the end of the month I'm running low on money, the manager will say, "Here's some money to get something. Just give it back when you pay your rent."

My parents, I don't want them to know everything. I remember when I told them I had HIV. My brother laughed. My father just lost it and told my brother that's nothing to laugh about. He came to my defense. You know, my parents are more compassionate than my brothers and sisters. In June I told my mother, "I've been drinking too much. I need to go into the hospital." She said, "Go. Don't be ashamed of that. You're mentally ill. A lot of people have mental illnesses." She tells me I shouldn't be ashamed of that either.

I ADMIRE PEOPLE WHO COME BACK AFTER ADVERSITY, PEOPLE WHO CAN BE IN THE GUTTER ONE DAY AND HAVE THE STRENGTH TO PULL THEMSELVES UP FROM THE GUTTER. SOMEBODY WHO HAS TAKEN THE WRONG FORK IN THE ROAD. NOT THE RAGSTORICHES TYPE. THE PERSON THAT HAS MADE IT DESPITE EVERYTHING ELSE.

As I said, my father is really sick and is going to go any day now. I can remember him being in the emergency room on the table and I go behind the curtain to see if he's OK and he's worrying about my stomach and telling me I should eat some soup. That's the kind of person he is. When my mother wasn't able to go the PTA meetings, he went.

My mother never worked. She just had kids all her life. And I remember I was five years old, I went to kindergarten half a day. And we would sit in the dining room and there would be chicken soup or tomato soup. And we would sit just all afternoon, maybe watch TV. We read books and we talked. Then all of a sudden she had another baby, and then she had another baby. Nobody wanted me around.

I wish I could wake up and say this was a dream, that I never had HIV, that I didn't get married, that I finished school, that I just didn't take so many turns. My life wasn't supposed to happen this way. I wish I had done something with my life. When you ask about what my day is like, my day is spent wishing that life wasn't like this. The next thing I know I'm going to be looking around and everything is going to be over. When I get my mental health together, then my body's going to fall apart. But look at me now. I'm a wreck.

Yeah, I feel lonely, but I don't know how else to feel. I like to listen to music, anything from Barbra Streisand to Aretha Franklin. I particularly like Phyllis Hyman. She's a Philadelphian. She died in '95. She was a modern Billie Holiday. Her songs are "I Refuse to Be Lonely," "I Want to Get Back to Paradise," music where she's lost herself, lost her self-respect, and she's telling us she refuses to be lonely.

I wish I could go out and forget about my HIV and have me a good time before it's too late, as the song says. A side of me wants to take care of myself. A side of me, when I get depressed, is self-destructive. I won't hurt anybody but myself.

I admire people who come back after adversity, people who can be in the gutter one day and have the strength to pull themselves up from the gutter. Somebody who has taken the wrong fork in the road. Not the rags-to-riches type. The person that has made it despite everything else. Natalie Cole, who went through drug addiction, that's the kind of people that I admire.

Sometimes talking about my life is a little bit of relief. It helps me to search for words to describe what's going on inside. I'm forced to look at myself. Things come to mind that I never thought about that maybe really are affecting me. A little relief, like when you take a breath of air.

SEANA O'FARRELL

Seana O'Farrell

WHEN MAGIC JOHNSON had tested positive, I just got this real sinking feeling that HIV was one thing that I needed to be afraid of. It wasn't that I identified with him. It was just this voice inside me saying, "Oh my gosh. You need to be careful about this." It was almost like a premonition. But I just kept on living my life.

I don't know when I was infected. As far as I know it could have been the very first time I had sex. I had to be infected through sex because I've never used drugs.

When I finished high school, around the time my parents divorced, it was a hard transition. I tried to make a new community of friends. I went to night clubs to meet people. I got attention through sex. I just felt that I had to have sex to be liked and to be worthy and I didn't know how to discuss condoms and I didn't know how to say no. I thought that if I had sex with someone, they would find out what a wonderful person I was and that they would come back and they would fall in love with me and we would live happily ever after. And it never worked that way. I guess my thing was I just didn't feel good enough about myself to find love within myself.

When I went to my Catholic high school in San Jose, California, I vaguely remember some HIV education, but it really didn't make such a impression on me because I didn't start having sex until after high school. Through the media what I was seeing was that HIV was a gay disease and that it didn't affect people like me. And it was never discussed in my circle of friends or with my sexual partners, ever.

So after high school, when I was nineteen, I went to Fresno to live with my grandmother and to go to school. My mom and I weren't getting along very well. My dad moved to Fresno shortly after I did. I got a degree in legal assisting from a business college and I was planning on settling down in Fresno.

When I was twenty-three I got pregnant and was planning on having the baby. I had discussed this with my mom and with the father of the baby. And he wanted nothing to do with it. My mom was very supportive. I figured that I had a full-time job, I was working at an insurance company with excellent benefits, and I had a degree, and I just felt that I was responsible enough to handle that even if I was doing it alone. My cousin had just had a baby the year before on her own, and I just felt I could do it too.

What prompted my AIDS test was that it was offered to me as one of the prenatal tests. I opted to get it, but I really didn't think HIV was something I needed to be concerned about. I went back a few weeks later for my prenatal exam and that's when they gave me the test results. There was a woman sitting behind the desk. I saw a pamphlet on her desk that said "HIV and Pregnancy." I saw it and I knew. And that's how I found out. So then she confirmed the fact that the test had come out positive. Of course I was totally shocked and could not accept it at all.

Then this doctor who was head of the ObGyn Department said to me, "Now we have to discuss what we are going to do about this baby." I didn't know what all of it meant. She told me a lot of "facts" that I found out later weren't actually factual. For example, she said the chances of transmission of HIV to the baby were like 60 percent and it's actually much lower than that. She also told me that carrying the baby could put my health at risk because the baby would drain all the nutrients that I needed to fight the HIV. And so I believed her and they scheduled me for an abortion the next day. I don't think they should have pressured me to have the surgery the next day after getting such horrible news. I went to the doctor on Monday, had the abortion on Tuesday, and Thanksgiving was on Thursday. It was a busy and sad week.

WHEN I FINISHED HIGH SCHOOL, AROUND THE TIME MY PARENTS DIVORCED, IT WAS A HARD TRANSITION. . . . I THOUGHT THAT IF I HAD SEX WITH SOMEONE, THEY WOULD FIND OUT WHAT A WONDERFUL PERSON I WAS AND THAT THEY WOULD COME BACK AND THEY WOULD FALL IN LOVE WITH ME AND WE WOULD LIVE HAPPILY EVER AFTER.

I totally put all my trust into this woman. Doctors were like God to me. I'm not sure even if I had been told the accurate statistics back then if I would have decided to have the baby. It's definitely something you have to think about. But now that I've thought about it for a whole year, I can say that I would have had the baby.

After getting over the initial shock of my HIV diagnosis, I tried to lead my life normally. I went to work still. I still hung out with my same crowd of friends. I didn't tell them what was going on. Now I've actually lost contact with all those friends from Fresno. They were kind of shallow, superficial friendships, kind of where I was at the time.

When I got my first bad cold, I freaked out and thought, "Oh my gosh, I'm going to die. This is it." And so that's when reality hit me and that's when I went into a depression and I started having anxiety. And that's when I felt really alone. I made the decision to move back home, to live with my mother in the San Francisco Bay area, because

I knew I needed a support system. I also thought there would be more resources for me there.

While I was still in Fresno, I began seeing a psychologist three to four times a week. That's how bad I was. I was going through anxiety and panic attacks and stuff. She got me through some real rough times.

Now physically I feel great. I feel healthier than I did before I tested positive just because I do take care of myself. I do get my rest and I eat healthier and my attitude is better.

There is a lot of positive attention on protease inhibitors, that they're doing a lot of wonderful things for a lot of people. But there is still so much that we don't know about them. So I'm a little skeptical. I've had people in the HIV community, positive people, yell at me saying, "You should be on medication. You're living in denial."

My mom gets kind of mad at me sometimes because I spend a lot of time wishing that my life could be like it was in the past. My old lifestyle, although it wasn't very healthy, was so simple. I went to work, I paid my bills, I came home, hung out with my friends. I really didn't give "life" too much thought. I'm trying to get past that.

Since I got a handle on my anxiety, now I can look into the future. But they're real short-term goals. Getting a job, getting a new car and that sort of thing. It's kind of difficult though, because, like, my mom's friends will come over and they don't know what's going on. And they've got kids my age and their kids are going to school or they're working in their careers. They ask me, "Well, what are you doing?" I want to say, "Well, I can't have what your kids have. I look at life in a different way now." I would like everyone to know about my situation just so that I could get it off my chest, so I don't have to be dishonest about it. But telling them is a whole different story.

I REALLY BELIEVE THAT ATTITUDE HAS A LOT TO DO WITH GETTING INFECTED. IF YOU DON'T FEEL GOOD ABOUT YOURSELF, THEN YOU BECOME A RECEPTACLE FOR HIV. . . . SO I TRY TO MAINTAIN A POSITIVE ATTITUDE AND KEEP AS MUCH ANXIETY AND STRESS OUT OF MY LIFE.

It's real difficult to make friendships in the HIV community. We're all dealing with such different aspects of the disease. But I've met some wonderful people in the HIV community that have turned out to be really good friends, much more so than my old friendships, because we have nothing to hide. Our most intimate things are out in the open.

My mom is a big part of my community. We went to this intense weekend-long seminar about treatment, exercise, and the emotional aspects of support. My mom was a real oddity there. By the third day everyone was so bonded and so close. They were crying and saying how lucky I was to have my mom there. A lot of those men are gay men that were first disowned when they came out as gay, and when they got HIV, well, forget it. Their mothers weren't there.

My father doesn't know about my situation. We don't have a very close relationship. I was sixteen when he moved out of my house, so his views of me are still like I'm a sixteen-year-old year old. He's probably still thinks I'm a virgin. To tell him about this would really blow him away.

I would like to reach out to young people. Of course, I'm not the kind of person to tell them, "Don't have sex at all." But I believe if you give them tools and insight into why they don't need to have sex, then hopefully there will be other possibilities. I believe we need to teach condom use and we need to promote safe sex, but I think also that's not the root of the problem.

I really believe that attitude has a lot to do with getting infected. If you don't feel good about yourself, then you become a receptacle for HIV. If you are living a healthy lifestyle and you feel good about yourself, you can have sex and you won't be a receptacle for it. It's kind of a belief that my mom and I share. So I try to maintain a positive attitude and keep as much anxiety and stress out of my life. Lately I do feel a lot better about myself.

It's almost like people are going back into the closet about their HIV. When the protease inhibitors came out in 1996, there was hope and excitement in the community. People felt safe to be out about their status. They were going to be healthy and lead normal lives. Over the past few years, people see that the drugs are not as glamorous as everyone thought they were going to be—there are problems of side effects and compliance and availability. So people are not feeling as safe to be out about their status. I have been working for Bay Positives, a nonprofit that serves youth with HIV and AIDS. We are having trouble finding young speakers with HIV who are willing to be open about their status. This didn't used to be the case.

My four-year testing anniversary was just last week. I haven't had to go to the hospital in all those years. I am very thankful that I have been healthy. My mental health has always been my biggest challenge. I still struggle with anxiety. I would like to be able to function better than I am able to now. I would like to be able to travel and be more involved and social. I would like to go back to school.

Every day I just have to tell myself, "I can do it." It would be much easier to just stay at home in my safe space. But I developed many tools so that I can get myself through the day.

Looking back, I see that with my diagnosis I lost my innocence. Before I was going through my life thinking I was invincible. I was just going to live forever. I had nothing to be worried about, and I was in control of everything around me. Then my diagnosis came and I realized that I am going to die. Not tomorrow. But it's just this certainty of dying that I didn't have before. This is the loss of innocence. It's really hard to explain unless you have been through it.

Edward L. Kingsley

WE'RE IN the Yucatan Valley in rural Minnesota, not too far from the Wisconsin border. I own thirty acres on this side of the road. Hills all the way around, wooded areas, gravel roads. I discovered this log house when I was looking for a place to build. Ended up taking it on as a challenge. This was nineteen years ago. Before that I had an eighty-eight-acre farm not far from here.

Yes, I'm a country boy at heart. I grew up on a dairy farm about fifteen miles from here, on the other side of the river. The only time I've lived anywhere differently is when I was in the service.

I'm a Vietnam veteran. Flew support missions out of Guam, in supply, 1965 through '67. That's how my daughter came into my life. When I was over there I helped move an orphanage. Just seeing all those babies. When I got back from Vietnam I married my childhood sweetheart. We had a son of our own. We adopted an Amerasian girl. I felt that was one thing I could do that was positive because I was against the war. She was only a couple of months when we got her. She's thirty-two now, a school psychiatrist out in California.

Our biological son is thirty-four and lives nearby. He's a contractor. He has a son, so we have one grandchild and one step-grandchild. My ex-wife lives nearby. So do my mother, a sister, and three brothers. My father died in '83, before my AIDS diagnosis. That was good that he didn't know.

I've been married twice. My first marriage lasted eleven years and three days, I was single for eleven years, my second marriage for exactly eleven years. And I tried to have a gay relationship. I consider myself bisexual. At this time in my life and probably the rest of my life it's abstinence.

I got my HIV diagnosis right before my second marriage, so it would be around '87. When I was single I got caught up in sex, drugs, and rock and roll. I slept with both men and women. And then I shot up for about a year and a half. Used dirty needles. I believe that's how I contracted HIV. For a long time it was alcohol, then cocaine. You could party in Rochester or LaCrosse or the Twin Cities and find all sorts of stuff.

It's got to be six years that I'm not working. I'm fully disabled. Mostly my struggle is with my right side, paralysis, getting weaker all the time. That's from an accident I had as a young man, diving into a swimming pool and hitting the bottom. Maybe the HIV is making it weaker too. I'm on a drug cocktail right now. I've had some tiredness and have gone through night sweats at times.

What is it like living in the country with HIV? All my neighbors know I'm positive. All my friends and family know. The barber at my local village knows. He will ask me how I'm doing. Have I gotten really sick lately? Do I have full-blown AIDS? I think is what he is asking. That's the more scary part, I think, for people that don't know much about HIV.

I'm the only HIV positive person in this county that I know of. In the next county there are three or four. There's basically nothing for anybody around here that's HIV positive except for RAN [Rural AIDS Network], which is a network of volunteers.

EDWARD L. KINGSLEY

I've always told myself that I wasn't one of these people that was going to let HIV make me move to the city so that I could be around other HIV people. So I go to a support group in LaCrosse, about forty-five minutes away. There are HIV people who come to my place on a pretty regular basis. I help people get sober. There's a high rate of alcoholism and drug abuse in HIV.

Last winter was a harsh winter. I didn't want to drive out of here and I just let fear take over. Even though I have a cell phone in my car I was worried about being stranded. So I stayed home a lot. I went through a lot of real deep loneliness, experiencing it like I never had before.

The Amish help me. Fifteen miles from here there is a big Amish community. I do stuff for them and they do stuff for me. For example, yesterday it was me doing something for the father and then him having his boys help me haul hay. The family that helped me yesterday, their oldest son did most of the fencing here. I was with him when he got married and when his first child was born. I was with him one time when he got seriously hurt. And they know about me being HIV positive. They were not judgmental at all. They once had a drifter come through who had AIDS so they were experienced with it.

Other family and friends help. In the winter, because people are worried about me going up to the barn and getting stranded, three different volunteers per week would come down and help me with chores. Now I have a renter so that helps a little bit. One of my brothers just came down from LaCrosse and put in a vegetable garden for me.

My own family was shocked when I told them I was positive. They are tolerant but only because I'm from here, I'm local. And because I don't flaunt anything—like there's no triangular flag up by my mailbox or the rainbow flag. I wouldn't do that anyway. I don't want to be that political.

I think it's been hard on my mother. About three or four years ago during an AIDS weekend, the local television station did an interview of me and just showed the side of my head. My mother hated that I was doing that. A neighborhood lady saw it and said, "Oh, I know that was Ed on TV. I think it's great that he's doing that and speaking out." That helped her a little bit, to have one of her best friends say that.

Oh yeah. I'm in a community. It's not real tight, but then anything isn't always what you want it to be. In the country there is no overt hostility. They just withdraw. I had a younger brother who died at age forty of AIDS. While he was alive I kept my own diagnosis secret because I felt my family couldn't take two of us. I eventually did tell them about my HIV.

Looking back on my life, the biggest change was when I decided to go into the human services field. For many years I had worked in plastics—making colors for plastics. I wasn't happy working there. My alcoholism was getting in the way. I wanted to work with people. So I resigned my job and went through treatment. And that's when I started thinking about what's important in life.

SOMEWHERE IN ALL OF THIS, THE DESIRE TO FIND PEACE IS THE MOST IMPORTANT THING— PEACE WITH PEOPLE, WITH THE ANIMALS, TO HAVE THAT SENSE OF PEACE INSIDE ME.

At age thirty-seven I went back to school and took a nursing degree. It was a very interesting time. I worked at a home for alcoholics, and then I worked in detox. I also started writing about the country life, just for fun. I wrote a short story and it was published in a Rochester paper. The manager of a radio station saw the story in the paper. He ended up helping me open Sunrise, a recovery center. I was its first director. It's still going today.

I wish I could get motivated to put my short stories in a small book. One of my favorites is about taking my horse and buggy to an Amish funeral. I had bought a harness from an Amish man who was dying of cancer. His son, who knew I was living with HIV, asked if I would talk with his dying father. Then when his father passed away they called me up and said, "Would you like to come to his funeral?" There were about eighty-five other buggies there. I think the ending line in my story is, "You can be in a strange land with strange people speaking a strange language. But when people start crying about the loss of their loved ones, you know what that is." So we all have this connection, we are all people.

I'm the type of person that likes looking at the configurations in the bark of a tree and the leaves and all the terrain and absorbing it all, enjoying the smells, enjoying the changes, enjoying the animals—all of it.

It's amazing, the connection I have with the animals. Even the geese. When I had a pet deer, it was caught in the fence. It wouldn't drink anything for three days. I took a catheter up there and told him, "If you don't drink soon, you're going to have this shoved down your throat and it ain't looking good." And he stared deep into my eyes and drank. I carried him down here and watched the *Today* program with the deer lying on the couch next to me. It was a really beautiful thing.

I fell down the other day in the bathroom and couldn't get up for a long time because my legs are so weak. Then I thought about winter. "Ed, are you going to be able to do another winter here?"

So I have checked out assisted living and nursing homes. Everybody says I'm too young for that. And I think I would be socially isolated with the older people when they would find out I was HIV positive. Some days I'm stronger and tell myself I can hang on longer out here on the farm, and then other times I don't think I can do it.

I have Social Security disability. It's a lot to be grateful for. I get over $1,000. It's because I worked so many years and I had good-paying jobs when I worked. If I needed some extra medications or something, I might be able to go through veterans organizations. I have a really great doctor. My meds come out of Pennsylvania and they deliver to my front door. They make it easier to be here.

I think what makes me tick is involvement. It's kind of an energizer, fights off any type of depression, self-pity. When depression comes, it's really horrible. I listened to Christopher Reeve once and they asked him, "What was the hardest part?" He said the morning, when you're laying there and another day has started and all the demons are saying, "Can't do it." And there are times when I will momentarily give in to that, one or two hours. And then I say, "Go and do something, get going."

Somewhere in all of this, the desire to find peace is the most important thing—peace with people, with the animals, to have that sense of peace inside me. How much torment do you want to put into something before all of a sudden you say, "I can't change that" or "That's the best it can be." It's the serenity prayer. I probably say it a hundred times a day. If you're tormented, it's because you can't accept some people, place, or thing as what God meant it to be at that moment. That was what I discovered went wrong with my relationships. I wasn't accepting enough. It had to be my way.

I used to be such a perfectionist with my yard. Now other people mow it for me. It's not like I mowed it. But you come to the point where you accept what it is and let go.

I planted all the trees you see, every one of them. I wanted to someday sit underneath them all. And here I am. But it's not the way I thought I would be. I didn't think I would be partially paralyzed, living with HIV, divorced, and being so proactive. I listen to myself sometimes and wonder, how did this shy country kid come to speak out about HIV and AIDS?

STEVEN ISENBERG

Steven Isenberg

I AM THIRTY-NINE years old. I am considered a long-term survivor, someone who has been HIV positive for at least ten years and is still functioning fairly well. I was diagnosed with HIV in 1985, and I really didn't have any symptoms or worries until 1992. I've had some gastro problems, and I have had twenty-six treatments for the cancer on my lip. Up until '92 I still worked, I still traveled, lived a normal life. I was going to the gym every day just like everyone else and going to dinner. You looked at me just like you looked at someone else and boom, boom, who knew?

I had my own company since 1986, a manufacturer of children's clothing. And I worked hard. In 1992 I began to get opportunistic infections and my T cells went below 200, which at that time was the determining factor on whether you became eligible for Social Security and disability. I had to decide to either stop working, slow down, or keep going at the same pace. I decided to stop working when I realized that it just wasn't me to work part-time. I had a very good disability insurance policy, which I had taken out when I found out I was HIV positive. So I activated it in 1992 without any problem.

When I first stopped working, I didn't know what to do with myself. I was lost. Since then I have learned to appreciate simple things, like going to a park on a beautiful day. Now my values are a lot different than they used to be. I'm a lot more spiritual. I am studying the Kabala with a tutor.

I NO LONGER SEE PEOPLE WHO DON'T MATTER TO ME. I HAVE MY CORE GROUP OF FRIENDS, AND I WOULD SAY HALF ARE POSITIVE AND HALF ARE NOT. BUT IT'S DIFFICULT SOMETIMES WITH FRIENDS WHO ARE POSITIVE. THE THOUGHT CROSSES YOUR MIND, "ARE YOU GOING TO BURY HIM TOO?"

I'm much more content in a certain way, believe it or not, less anxious. I don't allow myself to get as crazed as I might have in the past. It's taken me a long time to feel that it's OK to be unproductive, even though you are being productive because you're taking care of yourself.

Probably the hardest part for me is asking other people for help. It's much easier being on the giving end of things than the receiving. I've always been the giver. And now when I need help, rather than ask someone to go to the store or come over and cook dinner, I'll order in food. That's always been my biggest fear with this illness—losing control of my life.

Right now I don't really need a whole lot, but, for example, a year ago I was having very bad stomach problems and I was on an IV and I was pretty well medicated and it was to the point where I really couldn't drive. So instead of having my mother or father fly out and take care of me, I hired an attendant to drive me around and take me to doctors' appointments and cook for me and do that kind of thing, which still allowed me to be in control.

I grew up in Michigan and came to San Francisco in 1981. I must have gotten infected during my first couple of years here. Back in Michigan I have a very large family and a lot of close friends, so Michigan feels like a safety net. I know that in a certain way I would almost like to be living back in Michigan at this point in my life. But I know I would not get the medical care that I get here, without a doubt. The doctors in San Francisco are cutting edge.

My father is a doctor and medical stuff doesn't scare me. I'm very astute medically. I research everything. I keep track of all my lab work. I read a lot of medical journals intended for doctors. There's a lot I don't understand, but I think I pick up bits and pieces. When I go to my physician I have a list of things to discuss. "Marv, what's this new thing? Explain this to me." I see my physician probably more than most people. I go every two weeks. Most of my friends go once a month. I feel more comfortable going more often.

I think surviving a serious illness has a lot to do with attitude, how much of a fight you give. I also think the medications I've been on have a lot to do with my survival—almost all experimental drugs, always the latest. Certain people might keep all their pills on their countertop. I don't. I have a pill drawer that is totally organized. Every night I lay out my pills for the next day. I don't want to be totally reminded 100 percent of the time. I'm not trying to live in denial, but I don't have to look at everything constantly.

Financially I'm in a position where I can pretty much do what I want to. I don't have to worry about having Project Open Hand to deliver meals. I can go out to dinner. I do Waiters on Wheels—delivery of restaurant meals—a lot. I mean I'm not extravagant either, and I give a lot to charity.

I go into schools as an AIDS educator. I always have good interaction with kids, and I don't feel intimidated to talk about this disease. I like talking to kids more than adults because they are more naïve and ask very interesting questions. There is a warmth to it. And an innocence. You can walk into a room with teenagers and walk out an hour later and really see an effect, whereas you can have the same talk with adults, and you might have affected them, but you can't see it, you can't feel it.

My hope is that the kids will take a little bit more time to reflect on what they might be doing in terms of risky behavior, which is real tough, because when I think back to when I was fourteen, if someone told me, "You have to do this, you have to do that," I would have thought, "Well, fuck you." I was very rebellious at fourteen. That was when I first used drugs. You think you're invincible at that age.

I didn't tell my parents I was gay until college. They were divorced around that time. My mother probably dealt better with it than my father. Now my mother happens to be very active in Michigan AIDS work, a lot of volunteer work, a lot of speaking. With my father I would say, "Would you please send a check for $1,000 to this organization?" And he would.

My routine now is I'm up at 6:30 A.M. I used to go to the gym every day. Physically I can't do that anymore. I go two times a week, maybe three. I have a personal trainer. I don't do as much weight as I used to. But that's OK.

Just being with certain people is real important to me. I no longer see people who don't matter to me. I have my core group of friends, and I would say half are positive and half are not. But it's difficult sometimes with friends who are positive. The thought crosses your mind, "Are you going to bury him too?" I had a support group of six people and just two are left. I find myself saying, "Why am I the lucky one?" And then I wonder, "Am I really lucky?" That's really the bottom line. But I find it gets sad because I've been losing more and more friends and I'm fearful of making new friends because I don't want to go through the grief. My therapist of seven years passed away about two months ago. I was angry at him. How dare he do this to me. How dare he leave me first.

I had friends who have taken their own lives ,and I give them a lot of credit because I don't know if I could do it. And then I've also had friends who have just lingered and lingered and have been skinny and in diapers and horrible to look at. They can't talk anymore. You want to do something but there's nothing to do. It hurts.

There are also times when I'm terribly depressed too. I will stay in bed for a week. I won't answer the phone, I won't take my medication. I pull the blanket over my head. I just escape. I don't do it as much as I used to, but I did the first couple of times I got sick. That's when they put me on lithium and a couple of other drugs.

I feel that having this illness has changed my life and made me a better person in a lot of ways. It's almost like having the emotional perspective of a sixty- or seventy-year-old who has experienced a lot and has friends that are dying, retiring, getting sick—all the things that are happening to me at thirty-nine years old. I mean, it's not supposed to be that way. By fast-forwarding, there's an aspect that includes growing up quicker, being less judgmental, doing what you want to do, not worrying about what everyone else is going to think all the time—a certain sense of power in terms of one's own destiny. There's a strength that comes with that, and that strength, at least for me, is one of the reasons I'm still here.

[UPDATE]

Steven Isenberg died three years after this interview.

LUIS DELGADO

Luis Delgado

IT'S BEEN A CONSTANT struggle with my life. But I guess it's for the best because I'm now the person that I am. The way I think, the way I feel, is because of what has happened. Certain things happen for a reason.

I'm twenty years old. I live with my sister and her two children in the Bronx. My sister is basically my father and mother. My mother passed away when I was four, when my sister had just graduated from high school. So she decided to take care of me and my brother rather than letting the state claim us and send us off to God knows what foster home. We've had our tough times but we've always pulled it together.

My father is Cuban. He was never around. He and my mother divorced. Now he has established his own life in Puerto Rico. I finally met him when I was nineteen. He acted like he'd seen me the day before. "Now that you've met me, let's just go on with life." I feel that's totally wrong.

My father doesn't know that I'm gay. He doesn't know that I am HIV positive. But there will be a time and a place where I sit down man-to-man and just talk to him. I have a lot of questions I want to ask him. I feel like many parents nowadays don't have a lot of understanding with their children. They don't sit down and talk with them.

When I was seventeen I came out to my sister that I was gay and to my brother when I turned eighteen or nineteen. I guess with any family member they take it kind of hard. It's not just that your child is a homosexual but it's dealing with the "out" world, trying to protect your child from all the ignorance that exists in this world. But I'm proud of the fact that they took time to be there for me.

Last year, right around this time, actually, when I was nineteen, I was diagnosed as HIV positive. I knew that there was something wrong with my body, that something internally was wrong. I'm the type of person who is really in tune with my body. So at that point in time I knew that I had HIV. I didn't want my sister to know, but she had found out regardless, because of she works as a nurse practitioner. She had drawn my bloods. When she found out, she was like, "I'm here for you." She tried to stay strong.

When I found out, instead of mourning, you know, which I think is normal for anybody, I kind of did the opposite. I wasn't going to have myself be brought down. So I was constantly trying to get my schooling together, trying to get a job, trying to get my life together. While I was doing all that I was hurting inside. I was really questioning all my beliefs, every aspect of life. I was trying to find an answer. "Why me?" I broke down. I went into a deep depression.

After a while I realized there's more to life than being at home, stuck in a room, looking at four walls, and trying to come up with an answer when the answer is just to live life. Basically I got tired of laying there and made a big effort to live life.

Finishing school is a big priority. I have one more year to go. I had dropped out of high school. It was just something I wasn't interested in at the time. I move at my own pace.

I got infected from a sexual encounter. I was ignorant, and at that time I didn't use a condom. You know how it is when you are young. You are in the heat of the moment when the opportunity is there. You say, "The hell with it, what have I got to lose?" Especially when that person is at the low point of their life. I wouldn't say I was so low, but I was going through a tough time.

I guess it was a death wish. I knew AIDS was out there. The way I saw it was, hey, you know I'm gay. It's most likely that nine times out of ten a gay person will catch it before anyone else. So what the hell. Excuse my language. I guess I really didn't give two shits.

Now that I have AIDS, it's broadened my way of thinking, my way of seeing the world. Now I feel there is a lot of things in life that I want to do. I want to tell others that it doesn't have to come to a point where it's death or an incurable disease to change their lives.

I would say my diagnosis definitely got me closer to my family. I cherish my family now. Before I took them for granted. It was ironic. My sister was constantly telling me, "Go to school, do something." And I told her, I still remember, that I have all the time in the world. God knows what could happen from now until my time of death. But I feel like I have a limited time. It's kind of like God smacked me in the face.

I hope that when my time comes, that I have accomplished what I have wanted to. Basically my goal in life is to study psychology and then to help youth in the ages thirteen and up.

I have a very open mind. I don't judge nobody. The way I see it, we are all human beings and we all have different goals and paths. We all live on one planet and everybody needs to get along with each other. As a human being that breathes the same air and lives on the same planet, who works hard every day, goes to school, walks, bleeds, smells, I deserve respect and deserve to be heard like everybody else.

AFTER A WHILE I REALIZED THERE'S MORE TO LIFE THAN BEING AT HOME, STUCK IN A ROOM, LOOKING AT FOUR WALLS, AND TRYING TO COME UP WITH AN ANSWER WHEN THE ANSWER IS JUST TO LIVE LIFE. BASICALLY I GOT TIRED OF LAYING THERE AND MADE A BIG EFFORT TO LIVE LIFE.

The ideal relationship for me would have trust and basically just accepting me for everything I am. When the person is down and out, I will be there for that person, no matter what. And when I am down and out, hopefully he will be there for me as well.

I'm always up-front. By being up-front you save yourself from having someone's blood on your hands. This is what I need from a person. This is what I'm willing to give to a person. This is what I am all about. Can you handle that? Actually I have met the first person that I want to establish something with. I've come out and told him my status. It was received well, but I had put up all my walls to basically prepare for whatever reaction that was going to take place. It was really good. Now the thing is I'm taking my time and my patience with the relationship.

It's really hard coming out to the person and saying, "Well, listen, I'm HIV positive." Nine times out of ten, especially in New York, the people will walk out on you or tell you not to call again or put you down. It's sad, it really is. I don't know how people could be so coldhearted. The next person you meet may not tell you they're positive and you will not know. And I know people like that. They've been with a person for five years and they still haven't known about their partner's status.

My support group at Mt. Sinai [Adolescent Health Clinic] is like a family. There are about thirteen or fourteen in the group. I like it. We are always happy to see each other. Not only that, we just pour everything out, whether it's HIV related or not. Basically, whenever somebody is down and out, we always try to lift them up, try to keep them in balance, just to be there for each other. When I came over here to the Clinic, I found stability. I found this is where I belong. It's pretty cool.

In a weird way I speak to my virus. I tell it, "I know you are very smart, I know you are a living thing and I respect you. But in order for you to live, you need me to live. So I suggest you calm down." Truthfully, I don't think about HIV every single day. For a whole year I haven't been on meds and my viral load has been stable and my T cells have been stable. I just live life. I just wake up and absorb it.

Penny

I AM TWENTY YEARS OLD. Right now I'm in a safe home, a group home for HIV kids. I have been there for a month and two weeks.

The group home is fun. There are just ten of us. I like it. It gives me a lot of support. A lot of kids have the same problems as me and we get to talk about it. Sometime we just catch up about anything.

Most of the people in my group home got HIV from having sex. But I was born with it, got it from my mother. She had AIDS and passed away when I was twelve. So I have had it for twenty years.

I was born in Manhattan, grew up in the Bronx. I have a brother and a sister. I'm the oldest. I did have another sister and she had AIDS too. But she passed away when she was four and I was five. When I was growing up my mother was there, but she wasn't there because she was running around. And my father was working and he also was an alcoholic so I was basically by myself with my brother and sister.

When I was seven they sat me down and explained that I have a lot of bad germs in my body and a lot of good germs. They called the bad germs a bad army. The good germs had an army too, but I didn't have a lot of soldiers in the good army to fight the bad army. So they said I've got to take these medicines to make more good soldiers to fight the bad army.

I had counseling ever since I was ten years old. That was when I got sick for the first time. I had pneumonia. They talked to me about HIV, how it's a disease and I can't do anything about it except to take these medicines. The first medicine I was on was AZT in liquid form, by IV. I would go to the hospital every month for that. Then when I started getting sick that's when they stopped AZT and I started taking other medicines in pills. I've been taking medicines for thirteen years.

MOST OF THE PEOPLE IN MY GROUP HOME GOT HIV FROM HAVING SEX. BUT I WAS BORN WITH IT, GOT IT FROM MY MOTHER. SHE HAD AIDS AND PASSED AWAY WHEN I WAS TWELVE. SO I HAVE HAD IT FOR TWENTY YEARS.

My parents got divorced when I was nine and I started living with my aunt. Then my father got remarried, so I moved back with my father and stepmother. She had kids and my father and her had kids so it's like eight of us now. And I'm the only one out of my family that has HIV. I felt like I was alone because I was the only one that had to take medicine every day, go to school, be in and out of the hospital. It was too much.

I was really close with my stepmother until I got SSI when I was eighteen. She started taking the money. I had to leave. So I went to live with a friend who has the same thing I have. I was dating her cousin and I didn't tell her cousin that I had HIV. We had unprotected sex one time. There was just a lot of problems so I left there and went back home. My stepmother was going to give me half of the money. But that didn't happen except for a couple of weeks. And so I left.

After that I lived with a couple of other friends. Then I was at my boyfriend's house. Finally I just went to a safe home. And that's where I am now. I'll be there until I get my own place.

But now I'm stable. Got counseling. Got a good caseworker. I told them not to look

PENNY'S SELF-PORTRAIT

for little apartments right now because I want to stay in the group home for a year, get the support, so that when I do go on my own I could be square enough to keep my apartment.

I go to high school in the Bronx. I'm doing math, government and economics, and English. This is my last year. I just want to graduate. Then I want to go into computer technology training.

I used to go to another high school. I told this boy that I was messing with what I had and he take it the wrong way and he told everybody in the school "Oh, she got this. She got that." They don't know how I got it. They just claim I got it from sex. "She's probably sleeping with this guy, that guy. She probably got more than just HIV. She got other stuff." So I had to leave that school.

I have a lot of friends. Some know my status, some don't. I have a lot of HIV friends. I have other friends that are real close that don't have the disease. Some people would probably treat me differently if they knew. Some of them would be oversupportive. Some would just be OK with it.

I like to party, go shopping or just staying home, going to the movies. I like all kinds of music—classical, hip-hop, rap, reggae, country.

Three wishes? I wish my mother was alive, healthy. I wish I didn't have HIV. And I wish to have a good family. It would be me, my husband, and my child and a house with a dog and no problems—no bills, no health problems, living normal. My husband would be there for me, he would take care of his child, he would cook, clean, be an understanding person, respectful, not violent, loving, sweet, honest. That's it. And my child would be sweet, nice, honest, not a little brat. We would just be a nice family. I have had boyfriends but I broke up with them because they cheated on me and had disrespect for me.

They say it seems easier because I've had this disease all my life. I say it seems easier for me because I don't have to worry about who I got to kill. Because I already know my mother gave it to me.

Luana Clark

I'LL BE FIFTY in a few months. I have two biological children, a son and a daughter. I also have a twenty-two-year-old adopted son. My best friend died of AIDS, and I have adopted her son. He and my daughter live with me now. My older son lives in Virginia with his wife and six babies, my grandbabies.

In 1985 when I started seeking help for my drug addiction, that's when I found out I was HIV positive. When you went through treatment, you had to go to the hospital where a doctor made a complete examination. On my chart was that I had been a drug abuser, and the doctor asked me if I would like to take the test [for AIDS]. I said yes, signed the paper, and took the test. And bing, bang, there it was. The person who took my test told me I would die in a week. At the same time she told me to get my will and stuff done because I might have six months, the longest would be a year.

I was devastated. I was in a treatment center, and not having any information except that AIDS kills, I thought if I was going to die I might as well die high. What was the use of getting clean? I tried to relapse. I was in the middle of the street, completely gone. But the good Lord intervened then. When I came to my senses I was in the middle of the street and Sister Augusta O'Reilly was holding me. The only thing I remember was that she was holding me so tight that I couldn't breathe. And that brought me back. And that's when my journey began.

I didn't do anything about my HIV status for five years. Just stuck to my recovery. I mean, I stuck to it like glue. While I was doing that, I was learning about the other disease, AIDS. At that time it was real difficult because there were no women coming out, no women talking about it. I was made a suggestion to go to a support group, and it was only myself and another white girl. I sat there and listened and learned. I got upset because there was nothing said about women with HIV.

I took all the trainings and then I became a facilitator for support groups, one for the newly diagnosed. My motto was, "You can live in spite of, not die because of." Then I had an all-women's group. Then I had a group for grandmothers who were the mothers of people who died. So I got a lot of fulfillment out of that.

I couldn't understand why the government was allowing women to die now that they knew women were getting infected. I don't know their reasoning. I needed to know who to talk to about this. I ending up going to Washington to see all of them people up there for the reauthorization of Ryan White. I ended up on the speakers' bureau for the National Organization for People with AIDS.

I got infected from either sex or doing my drug addiction. I used drugs from age eleven. I went from alcohol to smoking weed to coke. Never tried crack. Crack came on the scene way after my recovery. And then I tried heroin.

I've been blessed because I used before, during, and after both my kids, and only by the grace of God they're not sick; they wasn't damaged in any kind of way because

L U A N A   C L A R K

of my drug use. I did go to my prenatal care, and I did let them know that I was using. And so they saw me on a weekly basis. Back then there was no such thing as AZT for women or the babies. Thank God, my children are healthy. Maybe I wasn't infected when I was pregnant. I don't know. Could have been after my pregnancy because I did sell my body for drugs, or for money to get drugs. I was just down as far as I could go, and there was no other way but up.

I'm bisexual. I have a significant other. She and I have been together ten years. She's also infected. She still uses. I mean, she was clean for two years and she found out she is HIV positive and she's been struggling ever since. She has her own place now. I know I have to let her do whatever she needs to do. When she says she wants help, I give her a referral. I don't do it myself anymore. I had to step off to let her grow like I grew. I used to think I could change her. When it finally got to the point where she was taking things from my children, that's when we couldn't live together. Since that separation and my new relationship with the God of my understanding, what I'm doing is stepping aside, doing what other people did for me.

I am on medication now. I'm on what they call "salvage therapy." I got the side effects, like, I have drug-induced neuropathy. My vision is slowly but surely going. I have my cane with me. My right side is going numb, and I fall down a lot. My hands are starting to shake. I've had shingles twice. I've had PCP pneumonia twice. I'm clinically depressed—one of the side effects of the drugs is depression. My memory comes and goes at any given time. That's why I always have a pencil or pen, to write things down. My viral load is off the hook but it's not going anywhere. So that's the only glimmer of hope I have. This obesity is a side effect too. It's going to go all the way around my middle. So that messes with me as a woman, a vain woman. I like to look good.

I have stopped going to funerals. The ones that was in recovery that had AIDS— they were steady dying. All my friends were dying. And I'm saying these were good people and they were doing good work, and why did God take them instead of taking somebody like me who was not contributing to life? I was being treated for survivor's guilt. I had that real hard, real deep. That's when I started seeing a psychologist. I'm getting much, much better with that. For my mental health I don't go to hospitals to see my sick friends. I'll send them flowers or cards. I know they can see and feel how hurt I am when I come to visit them, and I know there is nothing I can do for them. It's just a matter of time. When I was hospitalized last November, my family and friends came to see me. I said, "Oh man, I can't be around them because I am putting them through unnecessary pain." I was hospitalized three times. Three times they told me I was going to die. And three times I told them I wasn't going to die. When you have AIDS, everything is dramatic one hundred times fold.

My story is my purpose for living. I believe that's why God had me go through what I went through. I am supposed to be a walking testimony to those who are still using that you don't have to live that way. And even if you are infected, you can have a quality of life and a successful life without dying.

About my children, I hope that this pandemic is history for them. I hope when my daughter starts having her own kids, and my grandbabies from my son have their kids, that they will see a cure for AIDS and it won't be a threat to them. That's what I want to see for my family and for the rest of the world.

I want my kids to be open-minded, leaders not followers, compassionate, a lot of love in their hearts. Not to be "punks." I have put them through everything. None of them have used drugs. Could be because they saw what they did to me. They say they are proud of me.

My mother is my number one fan. She's sixty-five and she's sickly. She hung out with me all day yesterday. I went and took her to have her hair done. Then we went where I was working on a proposal. She is a computer genius. We caught the bus and

I WAS HOSPITALIZED THREE TIMES. THREE TIMES THEY TOLD ME I WAS GOING TO DIE. AND THREE TIMES I TOLD THEM I WASN'T GOING TO DIE. WHEN YOU HAVE AIDS, EVERYTHING IS DRAMATIC ONE HUNDRED TIMES FOLD.

we ate and we talked and laughed and I went and did work and I sent her home. That was a good day.

Our relationship didn't used to be good. One time when she came to my house, I locked us in the house and wouldn't let her go. I just spilt my guts. Everything that I thought she did wrong, I got it all out. She slung snot. I slung snot. We cried and cried and cried. I kept her hostage for two days. On the third day I said to her, "If you want to go home, you can go home." She didn't want to go home. She told me things about her life that I had no idea of. And that's when our relationship started, 'cause I forgave her. Those two days were a blessing. And we've been the best of friends ever since.

I didn't mean to get mushy.

My future? I put a short-term goal always hoping for the long term. That way I won't set myself up for failure or disappointment. I want to enjoy my grandbabies and my family while I am healthier. My grandbabies are my precious little things.

Jerry Peterson

I KNEW I WAS GAY from junior high on. In college I was very closeted. I was quite involved with this Christian religious youth group called the Navigators. They're a lot like Campus Crusade, very Baptist type. I think the group gave me stability but it didn't help coming out at all. But it sure was nice as far as good friends. After my early twenties I did come out completely to my entire family. But I didn't flaunt it either.

I figured that I became infected when vacationing in Mexico early spring of 1995. I was out in the clubs having a good time and found an attractive younger adult flirting with me. I was very excited that he took an interest in me. Anyway, in the excitement and under the influence of alcohol, safe or safer sexual practices were not adhered to. As soon as I got back from my vacation, I had symptoms. Several months later I tested positive.

Most of my life I've lived in Minnesota, and most of my adult life I've been in Faribault. We're a small town, nineteen thousand people, about fifty miles from Minneapolis. Faribault is a stereotypical religious community for the extreme right. So being gay isn't OK and having AIDS isn't OK. But the community is changing. There is a large Latino and Hispanic population that is moving into Faribault. There are churches trying to take those cultures in. So Faribault is hopefully becoming more tolerant. But I'm always surprised by the kindness and warmth that people have.

I have a lot of family that lives in this town. Mother, stepfather, a couple of sisters and a brother, in-laws and nephews and nieces. When a younger sister of mine divorced, she left her three kids with her ex-husband. The welfare system stepped in and took the kids away. Eight years ago I volunteered to be foster father to the oldest one. He was sixteen. Now he's going to school at the U of M. A big tall kid.

A year later I volunteered to take the other two children. At that time Nathan, the youngest, was ten, and Mary was twelve. When they moved in, my friends at work threw a baby shower for me. Balloons and gifts. It was a lot of fun. So I became a parent and never planned on that. I do have a degree in elementary education and I taught for a very short time and discovered it wasn't for me. I just didn't have the patience.

Yes, my life really changed when I became a parent. Before the kids, I had a real sporty Geo Storm, which is an economy sports car. You could get two people in comfortably. Then I got the kids and I got a Dodge minivan, a "family car." Very opposite of what the young stud guy wants. That was a reality check.

I had to learn how to be a parent. I have sisters with kids, and my parents are nearby. They all helped. For example, Mary was twelve turning thirteen, so she was going to experience womanhood soon with her first period. With me being just a guy, I wasn't going to be prepared for it. My mother and my sisters told me that when she does tell me about her period, we should make a party, celebrate her womanhood. So when she told me I said, "Oh, you're a woman now." Took her out to dinner, got the stuff she needed and talked about it and she was very comfortable talking to me.

JERRY PETERSON

I didn't want to be a parent like my stepdad was. He was very critical and didn't give a lot of positive feedback. But I think I have been pretty good about telling the kids that I love them. I make sure I do that. They call me Pete. I tried to get them to say "Uncle Pete," but they never did. Most people assume I'm their dad. Like when I take them to the doctor, they know I'm their uncle but they'll say, "What does your dad think about this?" It makes me feel special.

In 1995, a year after the kids moved in, I got my AIDS diagnosis. When I tested positive I wasn't sure I was going to be able to manage the kids. So it was kind of like, "We'll see how it works." Initially I didn't tell them about my diagnosis because they were young and I didn't want to worry them or fear if their peers found out. Not much time passed and I told them.

When I was diagnosed, I was told I had three choices to go to for HIV care: one clinic in Rochester, about sixty miles from here, and two clinics in the Twin Cities. And my doctor was quite up-front about being uncomfortable with the diagnosis—not that he was worried about himself, but he was worried that he would screw up. He wanted me to see an expert.

After my diagnosis I continued to work in human services. I managed a couple of group homes for developmentally disabled adults. I told my immediate supervisor about my diagnosis because she was also my friend. She thought I should tell all the others at work. I kind of wish I hadn't done that because people assumed the worst and got too mushy or emotional and I wasn't ready for that. Some people were already guessing that I had AIDS because I had lost a lot of weight very quickly. At my max I weighed 205 pounds. Currently I weigh 130.

I stopped working in 1999 when I had a heart attack. I had a quadruple bypass. That scared me more than the AIDS thing.

Initially living here was very isolating. There aren't any life enhancement programs here like they have in the Twin Cities, like theater tickets, buddy programs. Even though Minnesota AIDS Project is this huge organization with headquarters in Minneapolis, they seem to have brakes right at the edge of the suburbs.

But for the last couple of years I have been involved with a local AIDS group called CHAIN—Caring about HIV and AIDS in Northfield, which is about fifteen miles away. It's a group of volunteers trying to help people who are infected in our area. Through that group I met another man who is HIV positive. He's an important friend to me. So we get together every Friday and we talk about whatever is on our minds. And once a month we drive to a support group that meets forty miles away in Mankato. We've been sponsoring a movie day at my house because I have a big-screen TV, so the support group from Mankato has been coming to my house every other month. We have a massage therapist come. And the CHAIN group funds the refreshments. I think that a lot of people with HIV and AIDS isolate themselves. You need contact with other peers, other than your brothers and sisters, your kids.

WE HAVE MADE A FAMILY—THESE WONDERFUL KIDS AND THEIR GAY UNCLE WITH AIDS.

The reality is I'm depressed a lot and it's really hard to have goals. A lot of times I just want to feel good that day. I'm very tired and sleepy the majority of the time. In fact, one of my meds is a stimulus to stay awake. It's either that or sleep all day and I don't want to do that.

I futz in my house. I own this triplex here and I'm always remodeling. This summer I replaced my deck and enlarged my doorway to my kitchen.

Even though I am more public about my status, I also can be very reclusive and mopey and really feel like there's no hope. So you can get these spurts of energy and then withdrawal. A good day would be doing something around the house and walking the dog. A bad day would be stuck on the couch watching TV or in bed sleeping. I really like it when I can do like we're doing now with this interview. I'm motivated and interested and I'm not worried about exposure.

My dog is a big part of my life. I spoil her rotten. The dog will just stare at me if she wants something. The kids are much more vocal about their wants. And teenagers want all the time. They want the car. They want everything. Another difference is you can leave the dog alone for the day but the kids, no.

It's ironic that Nathan, who had so many challenges growing up, had to move into the home of his gay uncle who has AIDS in order to find stability. Well, he's turning out to be a normal kid with a lot of good things going for him. We have made a family— these wonderful kids and their gay uncle with AIDS.

Ron Glasser

PEOPLE NEED TO KNOW the importance of wills and of expecting the unexpected. What happened to me could easily happen to others.

My partner and I were together for six years. He was older and did not have AIDS. I had a will leaving everything I had to him. He never expected to predecease me. He didn't have a will. He was a doctor who was very thorough in his work, but he never went to checkups for himself. He hated to go to the dentist. He was very absentminded as far as practical aspects for himself. And as I got sicker, I got more and more reliant on him.

He died of a stroke very recently. Very unexpected. Very difficult. He was only fifty-one. When he passed away, his estate discontinued my support. My partner was the heir to a big manufacturing family so there was a lot of money. I had relied on his promises of support. After his death his heirs were saying I was not affiliated with my partner and I was a casual acquaintance. There was a lot of character assassination. His family kept saying, "Well, he has AIDS and we don't need to support or be responsible for him." This was so wrong because my partner and I were totally intertwined. We had exchanged wedding rings, the whole thing.

So then I had to go to court to prove not only my relationship with him but my dependence on him and the fact that he had made these promises of support and that I had relied on them. And that's an enormous burden for someone to have to prove. There's not a lot of legal precedent for doing that. And here I had spent six years with this person, day and night, and we were each other's only family. His only other relatives were these out-of-state cousins he had never seen.

I had to sell everything, including an art collection I owned, to hire the lawyers. It's really cost hundreds of thousands of dollars to pursue that case, just to get that judgment. It was a brutal fight.

Gay people have no legal rights. Once you get into court, it becomes so apparent. When I went into probate court, because I wasn't a relative, I wasn't allowed to speak. My attorney couldn't speak because I had no standing. In probate court the judge said, "He doesn't look sick to me, and I'm sure his parents can support him." I thought this was so outrageous.

The trial court judge eventually ruled in my favor. It's a $160,000 judgment. Now the estate is appealing. The attorney said they're just waiting for me to die because my life expectancy is so minimal and they didn't expect me to put up such a fight. One of the reasons I want to put up such a fight is to prove that just because you have AIDS doesn't mean you are totally powerless. But it's really been a one-man sort of effort.

In '90 I found out I was sick. At first I sort of dismissed it or blocked it out of my mind. My partner was really in charge of handling all my medical. He supervised and paid for all of the treatments.

My own family is from Boston, Beacon Hill, very wealthy. I'm an only child. My par-

RON GLASSER

ents objected to my relationship and totally cut me off once I told them about it. They're going through a very messy divorce themselves. And they're both very paranoid of AIDS. They view it as a real stigma to have their Ivy League son have AIDS, a son who was supposed to be a hotshot lawyer in San Francisco. So my father doesn't talk to me at all and my mother only intermittently, when she has problems of her own. But that's just the way it goes. I don't dwell on it.

Growing up, we lived in a big brownstone, massive penthouse. My mother was very fearful of kidnapping, very overprotective. I wasn't allowed out of the house until I was seventeen, and I really hid being gay. And when I was eighteen I made sure I moved out, and my father got me another apartment. My life was all charted. I never really had a say in it. I wasn't happy. I didn't want to go to law school. That was more my parents' fixation. But I went through the motions. Once I finished law school, I worked for an insurance company.

My parents are very homophobic. My mother was so virulently anti-gay. She would always say, "Oh, those gay people should die since Hitler didn't finish the job." My mother says she really doesn't want to tell anyone I am sick because she doesn't feel it is anybody's business and there is no need to embarrass the family.

It's really the rush of events that has led me to be very agoraphobic and reclusive. When I found out I had AIDS, I did disclose it to my father. That's when my father totally cut me off. Once I did that, my partner had to pick up the pieces.

Now I'm totally destitute. I've really sent my father letters saying I'm very ill and really need some help financially. He just doesn't even respond. I just get Social Security and an SSI check and that's it. Medicare picks up medical bills which are mounting. It helps, but they only pay a portion.

There really isn't a community for me, and that's one of the reasons I wanted to do this interview. I feel it's such a farce about San Francisco being such a good place for people who are gay and especially those who have AIDS. In terms of my lawsuit,

I made requests to many organizations to help me with my suit. What was so ironic was that the firm who's representing the estate is an all-gay firm and they were using the argument "Well, they're not married. He has no contract. He's not entitled to anything." So I wrote to about twenty organizations, legal and social, and I said, "I really need advice about what to do. I feel isolated." And nobody even responded. Support from the gay community has just been nonexistent.

I don't feel the need to capitulate to the disease yet. I really don't want to give the people who are dealing with the legal situation the satisfaction of prematurely becoming deceased. I feel that would sort of play into their hands.

If I didn't laugh about it I'd really go out of my mind. Not too many people lose their career, lose their partner, lose their family, all within two years. I've totally withdrawn because I'm so convinced that if I go outside, something else is going to happen, another disaster.

My typical day? Well, it's sort of sad. I sit here on the sofa a lot. Until very recently a lot of my life has been primarily dealing with documents. Now I just sit and watch TV. I can't concentrate on reading. So it's pretty pathetic. I definitely don't use any intelligence I may have gained from all this education.

I would never go for a walk. I wouldn't want anybody looking at me or making judgments about me, like, "Oh, he looks sick." I'm not interested in interacting with other people because I've really been so disappointed that it's best to limit that to the absolute bare minimum. I haven't been to a restaurant or a movie since my partner died.

If I get the money from the judgment, my life probably wouldn't change that much now. I've been isolated for so long it would be fairly difficult to turn the trend. I don't think I'm going to rush out and start buying things again. I would want to save the money because it probably would be the only source of income I'd ever get for the rest of my life.

IF I DIDN'T LAUGH ABOUT IT I'D REALLY GO OUT OF MY MIND. NOT TOO MANY PEOPLE LOSE THEIR CAREER, LOSE THEIR PARTNER, LOSE THEIR FAMILY, ALL WITHIN TWO YEARS.

I feel this tremendous social stigma about having AIDS. Oh, absolutely. The majority of Americans view me as a leper.

When I thought about this book, I said, "Sure. There are going to be all those hopeful stories, about all these people doing Zen Buddhism, natural herbal, being in the mainstream of life." And then I said to myself, "Well, you're not really in the mainstream of life, you're not doing any of this, but on the other hand, you haven't gotten sick and you've been able to deal with all of this without completely losing your marbles." I thought there was a point to my story about self-empowerment, that even if you are sick, if you feel strongly enough about something, you can try to change the system. If I do win the appeal, the appeal becomes a part of case law, and then it will be cited in future cases. So I do feel part of trying to set the stage.

[FOUR YEARS LATER]

To bring you up-to-date about my lawsuit, the decision was decided on appeal in my favor. Eventually the judgment was paid. Once the attorney fees were taken out of it, there was little left. But it was more the principle than the money. I was pretty pleased that it turned out the way it did. It took about three and a half years to get the result—a long time.

There have been huge changes in my life since our first interview. When we first met, I could barely get up off the couch and definitely couldn't leave my apartment for anything except a doctor's appointment.

You probably weren't aware that I had a drug problem—speed, methamphetamine was the drug of choice—and that was something that I had not chosen to deal with. I guess a lot of my drug use had to do with being HIV positive and being alone and feeling such a loss of everything in my life. Eventually I went into recovery. It was a long, protracted process. I gradually built up my energy and my ability to deal with people and get out of the house.

RON GLASSER FOUR YEARS LATER

As soon as I got into recovery, I knew that I was working toward getting myself back. I had a flight plan, shall we say. I knew where I wanted to go, where I wanted to be. I needed to get that lawsuit behind me, and I needed to get off drugs, and I needed to clear my head. A lot of little steps.

I knew I wanted to go back to work. But the prospect of losing my disability benefits was really scary. I didn't know how I was going to survive if I was going to get sick, if I wasn't part of the state system. It required a big leap of faith, but I thought if I didn't take a job, I would just remain in the same niche. I might have benefits, but my life would be disastrous. I just did not want to sit around and live on disability. I needed something more challenging and directed.

GETTING A COMPUTER WAS WHAT REALLY CHANGED MY LIFE.

After a succession of different jobs, I ended up working in the collection litigation department of a major company in the Silicon Valley. I commute two hours each way by train.

Exercising came along with getting my life back in shape. I just decided to take my health and my physical appearance and my well-being under my own supervision. I go to the gym after work, so sometimes I don't get back in my house until 10:30 or 11 at night. And then I have to be up at 5 A.M. That's not a whole lot of time for sleeping.

I feel good. I am on protease inhibitors. My viral load went down to almost undetectable, and my T cells have stabilized. I'm pretty good about taking the medications and following the advice of my doctors. But it does affect how you feel—it makes one less energetic at times. I think that was part of the attraction to speed. It was a false sense that you could do anything.

Looking back on these past few years, getting a computer was what really changed my life. It helped me to become more social, to get advice from people who had similar experiences with HIV and losses. Otherwise I felt totally alone. Through the computer I hooked up with some people who were in recovery who suggested I go myself.

That sort of marked the beginning of this whole new change in my life. Interacting with people again felt good. And I didn't even have to face them in person!

I really stuck with the recovery program. Like going to meetings every day for a very long time. And I never relapsed. It's been, like, four years without a drink or a drug.

Now I have progressed to the point where the computer is part of my life. I work on systems all day and I download music. I talk to people on it, do my research on it, and shop on-line. And the person I've been seeing I met on the Internet. However, the odds of meeting someone you can connect with are not really great—sort of like horse racing, if you have enough time and patience to play the odds.

ANYA BLACKMAN WITH MATEO SOLTERO

Anya Blackman

I TESTED POSITIVE in July of '93 when I was twenty-four years old. Two weeks later I was given my first T cell count, and my T cells were 20. That really blew me out of the water. And so that's why I had this feeling that everything was about to end. Before I was tested, my health had seemed OK. I had some symptoms, but I didn't know what they were connected to. Like I bruised easily. I was really fatigued after my semester ended. Even my mom pointed out that someone my age shouldn't be so exhausted after a semester.

The day I got my results and those first few months—that was the hardest time I ever had in my life. Before my diagnosis, I was falling in love, I was doing well in school, I had just finished a tough semester, an internship and going to school full-time. So I fell from a really high place.

I am really close with my family. When I found out my results, my parents scooped me up and brought me back home for a while. They immediately bawled with me, they nursed me. They suggested I consider living at home for a few months. That helped me get back on my feet. Living at home, I didn't have to pay rent, so I quit the restaurant job where I was working at the time and quit school. Immediately, especially after the T cell count, I had to reassess everything. "Is it really worth my time if I don't know how long I have to live?"

NO ONE DESERVES TO BE INFECTED WITH HIV OR ANYTHING, WHETHER THEY WERE A GAY MAN OR A PROSTITUTE OR A CRACK ADDICT OR WHATEVER. IF WE LOOKED AT AIDS OR HIV AS BEING SIMILAR TO A COLD, THERE WOULD BE NO JUDGMENT ON IT. NO ONE SAYS, "HOW DID YOU GET YOUR COLD?"

A few years earlier I had gone to psychotherapy. I think this, plus my family, gave me a foundation to deal with my HIV. I also took a holistic health class, guided imagery and meditation. It was perfect. So all of these things helped me to bounce back.

At college I had been studying psychology and was one semester away from getting a B.A. I was always really interested in counseling people. I kind of had the idea—this was before I found out about my HIV status—that I wanted to be some kind of drama or dance therapist because those were my two major loves. And that changed because suddenly I didn't think I was going to have a future.

Right now I'm involved in the HIV community, and I've been told that I would be a great peer counselor to talk to other people who are infected, really from a place of understanding and compassion. I have been taking workshops on pre- and post-test HIV counseling. And I am also studying massage.

People ask me how I got AIDS and I tend to be a little guarded. Anyway, when I was nineteen I met this person who was ten years older than me. He had been a musician and was very cool. I thought I was in love and was really kind of taken by him. I was in the relationship with him for about two years on and off. Before we became sexual, he told me he was positive. I made the decision at the time that I was going to practice everything I knew about safe sex. I believed him when he said something was not risky.

I have since learned that "pre-cum" has a high amount of virus in it, and even rubbing and even rolling around outside the vagina is dangerous. I never really understood that. I thought it was just at climax that it was dangerous. And there were a few times where I think I was just a little sloppy in the safer sex habits. I was probably infected by him right toward the very end of my seeing him. He has since died.

There are different rings of the community around me, and my family is the tightest circle. Yes, they are great parents. Just to give you an idea, I blamed myself for having gotten infected. I really felt like I screwed up big-time. My parents helped to remind me that basically what happened was I took a risk, but it was a big, awful mistake, a big, awful accident. My parents were always there for me, calling to see how I was. And now, because I've been consistently well, they have given me more space. If my T cells have gone up by 10, they take me out to dinner. My mom will take time off from work to go to doctor appointments with me. My parents listen to NPR, and if they hear anything about HIV or AIDS or any new drugs, they're immediately calling me and giving me information.

I've created a new circle of friends who are positive or involved in the HIV community. I'm the receptionist and volunteer coordinator in an acupuncture clinic that specializes in HIV treatment. It's in a building with two other HIV-related businesses. So all around me are people who are positive or who know a lot about HIV. I've revealed my status to people I really like a lot. I'll be at the desk and one of the clients will come and we'll start talking about our side effects from medications: "Are you having firm bowel movements?" So I have a health community as well.

After my diagnosis dating became a nightmare. How do I tell? Could I tell? It just didn't go very well, and my heart was just breaking all over the place. You want to find love, you want to find that partner for life. And I really started feeling like I was given my scarlet letter and I just had to wear that for the rest of my life. I started to think I have to find someone who is positive. But just because you're positive it doesn't mean you are going to have other things in common.

I have a gem of a relationship right now and my faith in relationships is renewed! When I met Mateo nine months ago, I immediately liked this guy and he really liked me. He is not HIV positive. Right around the time we started kissing, I laid it out. We were taking a walk in the park, and I just told him. He just took it so well. Mateo is an intelligent person and he has his facts down. He had already known an HIV positive woman, just a friend, and so he had a lot of understanding of HIV. That was definitely a good thing. He is so responsible around my HIV, keeping himself safe. He is definitely the person I was meant to be with. It's so mutual. We're actually going to go look at engagement rings tonight! It just happens to be the night.

When I found out about my HIV, I immediately felt there was no such thing as any higher power, any universal life force or anything like that. I felt very fucked over by the universe. I actually said that many times. But over time I have been finding a more spiritual path. In some ways I feel lucky because this disease has given me a new understanding. The average person who doesn't have to deal with their mortality at such a young age doesn't get that understanding. When you don't know how long you have to live, you start treasuring people and treasuring things that happen.

Life for me has always been about learning, about growing, emotionally and spiritually. This whole HIV thing feels like a part of that. Sometimes I have really shitty days and I don't feel that spiritual. Generally if I have a cold or something like that, I go down on a spiral for a while. Or I think about not having kids and all that stuff. That's when this doesn't feel like a very spiritual path to me and I don't feel very lucky. At times I realize I'm a lot shakier on the inside than I appear on the outside. Mateo has been a real beam of light.

In the eyes of other people, there seems to be a hierarchy of ways people are infected—some ways seem to be more moral than others. One of my mother's closest friends died of HIV. She was infected through a blood transfusion. Well, she was the "angel" of people who are infected. I'm right after her.

I feel that sometimes when people ask me how I was infected, they have a need to categorize me. This judgment really gets me. Honestly, sometimes I even catch myself wanting to ask how someone was infected so I can categorize them. My deepest feeling is that no one deserves to be infected with HIV or anything, whether they were a gay man or a prostitute or a crack addict or whatever. If we looked at AIDS or HIV as being similar to a cold, there would be no judgment on it. No one says, "How did you get your cold?" It's really a bummer.

DONNA NATHAN

At the yearly retreat of our ten-year-old AIDS support group, we have a remembrance ceremony for those in our group

who have died. Those who are no longer here are sending me the strong message to live each moment with gratitude and grace.

All of my friends who have died are still a vital part of my life.

Donna Nathan

I LIVE IN THE fifth-richest town in Massachusetts. It's Republican, and as far as I know, I'm the only person with HIV in my town. But it doesn't stop me from disclosing my status. I'm not ashamed anymore.

My brother died of AIDS July 12, 1993. He was a homosexual and he contracted AIDS in 1980. The only thing that was available before he died was AZT. Yes, he suffered. He developed systemic tuberculosis, he went blind, he had dementia, he was in a hospital bed for forty days. He basically died of starvation. Unfortunately my mother was there and she kind of prolonged everything. She couldn't accept his dying. If I had control, I would have let the doctors give him some morphine.

At the time of his death I had learned I had AIDS too. I was diagnosed on February 7, 1992. The way I got it was a little more complicated. It was a string of sad circumstances. I'm bipolar [manic depressive] but I didn't know it at the time. A psychiatrist, a very incompetent psychiatrist, put me on Prozac.

The Prozac threw me into an extreme mania. I was working at an AIDS organization because of my brother's diagnosis. The director of that AIDS program asked me to be a buddy to a client who had AIDS. One thing led to another. I was reckless. I contracted it from a sexual encounter with this "buddy." He was very destructive, very evil. He was one of these people who was going to give AIDS to everybody he could.

My brother and I had sort of a pact that one of the ways we could curb this epidemic was to never give this virus to anyone. And to his death, he never gave it to anyone, not even to his partner of thirteen years. And I have never given it to anyone. That was our own personal commitment.

It wasn't until two years ago that I understood where my reckless behavior came from. That was when I was diagnosed with manic-depression. I feel kind of vindicated that now I have an explanation. It's not an excuse. I accept complete responsibility for my behavior, but I never understood why I almost sabotaged my good marriage. I have a long, good marriage. I've been with the same man for thirty-three years. I have two wonderful children. My daughter is twenty-two and my son's nineteen. There was nothing missing in my life.

After I contracted HIV, the psychiatrist took me off the Prozac and I became suicidal. He wasn't there for me. He was afraid I was going to sue him since my husband is a personal injury attorney. So I was kind of walking around for six years missing this piece of why and how.

My whole immune system had crashed. Within a year of infection I had an AIDS diagnosis. My doctor told me to put my affairs in order in 1994, when my T cells numbered 64. They called me a "rapid progressor."

What I was going through was like being in a shipwreck, an emotional and physical shipwreck. I came down with two major infections in two months. One was shingles, and the other was Bell's palsy, a facial paralysis which lasted for a month.

There were just so many levels of suffering. I was suffering from guilt and from shame and depression. And my bouts of mania and recklessness made my family suffer. It wasn't until my daughter was diagnosed with manic-depression that I started to do some reading, and finally with the help of a very astute psychiatrist we started putting two and two together.

Since I've been on treatment for manic-depression I've been able to go back to work—I teach English as a second language to adults in college. I feel like I've been able to regain some of my life back. It was after my fears and anxieties were under control that I could consider treatment for HIV. Because up until then, I didn't want to live. So now I'm doing well on the AIDS cocktail. My psychiatrist and my infectious disease doctor were on a conference call with me, and the psychiatrist said to my doctor, "I'm working on her mental health issues. Will you please work with her on her physical issues?" It was a team process.

PROBABLY THE GREATEST THING THAT I LEARNED FROM THIS DISEASE IS HOW IMPORTANT IT IS TO HAVE PEOPLE IN MY LIFE WHO ARE POSITIVE AND SUPPORTIVE. I TRY TO SIFT OUT THOSE WHO SUCK MY ENERGY AWAY. UNFORTUNATELY MY MOTHER IS ONE OF THOSE PEOPLE WITH NEGATIVE ENERGY. I'VE HAD TO DRAW THE LINE.

I really respect my husband for hanging in there with me. He's an intelligent, good, generous, and grounded person. He accepts my reality. Before I was on treatment for manic-depression, I had no perspective on what I had done to my family. Now I can look back and say, "My God!" I see that I was either in bed because of the depression or I was manic and never home. Now I can kind of sit back and see how he has been there for all of us.

My husband was eighteen when I met him. We have a long history together. I went to high school in Puerto Rico and I met him there. I think our relationship is in a really good place right now. Our daughter is now independent. She graduated college and is engaged. Our son is presently living at home and going to college.

I just turned fifty this year. As I am getting older, I see my friends who don't have HIV having to deal with physical and emotional issues. Now we're all dealing with perimenopause and menopause. We're just having fun being middle-aged ladies. I like middle age. We have lunch and do cultural things and go on trips. I like having time and energy and feeling creative.

My parents are seventy-eight. They don't have HIV and they don't smoke. I do. I never thought I would outlive my parents, but the face of this disease has changed so dramatically in recent years that maybe I will. It sounds like a cliché to say I just live one day at a time, that I live in the moment. But it's true. I mean, I blast my music, I dance in my kitchen, my puppy and I dance.

I think probably the greatest thing that I learned from this disease is how important it is to have people in my life who are positive and supportive. I try to sift out those who suck my energy away. Unfortunately my mother is one of those people with negative energy. I've had to draw the line.

I come back to the Mind/Body retreat once a year. It's always amazing how significant that experience is. I have a lot of heroes and support in this group. And then we do the remembrance ceremony for those in the group who have died. The striving to live is what we all have in common. The sense of humor and the struggle and the medical interventions that people allow to happen to them, the tubes that people carry around with them. The courage is the struggle to live, the same courage I saw in my brother as he lay in that bed for forty days.

At one point I emotionally and physically couldn't attend all the funerals of people I cared about. What I try to do with people who are very sick or are dying is to spend time with them while they are here.

There were times when I thought I was dying. Getting close to death dispelled a lot of my fears. As I confronted it, I was not so afraid. I used to insert needles into my brother's catheter to give him IV infusions. I was there, as close as you can get.

At some point I just figured that I had learned everything I could about death and suffering.

I have had a nine-year relationship with my doctor and I trust that he will not let me suffer if he can help it. I do not know what the circumstances of my death will be. None of us do. Right now I am busy living life, making plans and trying to stay grateful.

VINCE CRISOSTOMO

Vince Crisostomo

BOTH MY PARENTS are from Guam. They're Chamorros, the indigenous people of Guam, direct descendants of the Malays. My dad was in the U.S. Air Force. Growing up, the only consistent thing we had was that we moved a lot. I went to about sixteen different schools from grade one through twelve.

It was difficult for me in that I never got that feeling of belonging. I think I learned to never get attached to anything because for me it was always temporary. My looks—people didn't know if I was Chinese or Japanese—also made me feel I didn't belong. No one had ever heard of Guam.

I feel that I am a lot more Chamorro than I had thought, that certain personality traits that I have are very Chamorro. There is this whole respect for the land, the sea, the sky, this incredible relation-ship to nature. That's very much part of my people's culture, particularly my dad's family. In my mom's family, they have a very strong psychic spirituality, which I have some of.

What I have learned is that everything that happens to you is an opportunity. I can give you a very recent example which has changed my life tremendously. Three months ago I went to Thailand. All the news I had gotten of Thailand was very tragic by our standards. In a support group in Thailand you might have five hundred people—sex workers, families, mothers, daughters, grandfathers. Everybody has AIDS. But these people are very joyous. I think they feel pain, but for some reason they have made some sort of peace with that.

When I left Thailand, my plane ride back was thirty-six hours in transit. On the plane I was so tired I thought I was starting to hallucinate. I hadn't eaten well. I dreamed that I died. And what happened in that death was that it was very joyous. It wasn't horrible and I accepted it. In my dream the plane continued and took my body to San Francisco Airport, where my family arrived to greet me and claim my body. And at that point my spirit rose from my body and I saw my family coming in. And I told them, "Good-bye, I'm leaving. You know, it's been wonderful." I was totally accepting of what was happening.

And then I saw friends start to arrive and my spirit continued to rise above the crowd and I looked down and said good-bye to everyone. "This is over, I can go now. And my work is done." And so I had this incredible rush of joy, about to go to heaven. And I looked up and realized, I am not going to heaven. I'm going into the air conditioning vents! It was very dark. Finally I saw a light and started to move toward it and I ran into another air conditioning vent. And the stream of air pushed my spirit out of the vent and right back into my body. And I woke up and there was my sister.

When my spirit left my body and came back, my body was no longer heavy. There was a lightness that I will carry with me and that hopefully will guide me. I think I am wiser.

There are a lot of real sorrowful emotions that I have carried around with me for years pertaining to this epidemic. When my friends were dying at a fast rate, I couldn't comprehend and process it fast enough. And so as a result my body started to become very unhealthy. It has taken me a long time, but I feel I finally have accepted that this is my life. And I feel that this is going to be a long life and it's going to be a wonderful life.

I tested positive in '89. After that I had a sore throat which was actually a fungal infection in my digestive track. I developed food allergies and all the symptoms—night sweats, nausea. I couldn't keep anything down. I started to lose weight and I went down to 119 pounds. The doctor told me that it looked like a bomb had gone off inside my body and told me I had about six months to live.

After I got that diagnosis I came back to California and I expected to come out to my family. So I told my folks I was gay. I didn't say that I was dying. I never got that far because the gay part was so horrendous. My family disowned me. I think it is what I thought would happen and why I never told them before. And so I went back to New York. My mother wrote me a letter and told me I was not welcome to come home ever again. And she didn't speak to me for over two years. All my life I had been told I was loved, and it was like, "What did you love? Who was that person that you loved? It wasn't me."

But my father told me as far as he was concerned everyone was gay, some people just hadn't experienced that yet. It was totally not what I had expected. And it was funny because my dad and I were never close. But that brought us close.

> THERE ARE A LOT OF REAL SORROWFUL EMOTIONS THAT I HAVE CARRIED AROUND WITH ME FOR YEARS PERTAINING TO THIS EPIDEMIC. WHEN MY FRIENDS WERE DYING AT A FAST RATE, I COULDN'T COMPREHEND AND PROCESS IT FAST ENOUGH. AND SO AS A RESULT MY BODY STARTED TO BECOME VERY UNHEALTHY. IT HAS TAKEN ME A LONG TIME, BUT I FEEL I FINALLY HAVE ACCEPTED THAT THIS IS MY LIFE. AND I FEEL THAT THIS IS GOING TO BE A LONG LIFE AND IT'S GOING TO BE A WONDERFUL LIFE.

I stayed in New York and I started drinking and doing recreational drugs. I knew that would speed up the HIV and I thought maybe I could overdose or something else would kill me or I'd walk in front of a bus or something else would happen. My friends were all dancers, actors, or singers. Most of us worked in restaurants because that's how you made the money that also supported that kind of lifestyle. And then one night, when I was in one of the clubs, I, along with another friend of mine, was accosted by these six young high school boys in a limousine. And basically they bashed us. My friend got his head cracked open. And that was when I just heard this scream inside my own head. And that was when I figured out I had to get help.

I went to the Gay and Lesbian Center in the Village in New York. I met a counselor who was like a godsend to me. My intake took three hours. When it was done he just looked at me and smiled. It was the first act of kindness—no, the woman who gave me my blood test results after I tested positive was really nice to me—but this counselor just made sure I didn't get lost. To this day I am very grateful. I know how people get lost in this system. How it gets overwhelming and you just give up.

This counselor got me to support groups, referred me out to different agencies. At first when I went to the groups I would never speak because I was scared. And then I started to develop a voice. I learned about holistic health. I got to therapy. I learned about nutrition. I started to volunteer, and I worked with other people who were living with AIDS and HIV. Just the fact that he seemed to care so much kind of motivated me. I remember the first support group that I went to. Their spirits had already been sucked out of them. There was no fight left.

In 1990 I moved with my partner, Jesse, to San Francisco. Jesse soon became very sick, but my health was pretty good. And my mother and I did reconcile. One night at 1 A.M. in Jesse's hospital room, I was sitting on the cot—I stayed with him every night of his illness—and the door opened. It was my mom. I didn't want her to see Jesse at that point. He was so visibly deformed from his Kaposi's sarcoma, you couldn't even see the color of his skin because the lesions were so huge. My mom looked at Jesse and she said, "Oh my God, he's so sick." And she made the sign of the cross and she walked up to him and kissed him. I was in total shock. Once Jesse and I had gone to their house and she hadn't even come out to be with us. But in the hospital she took both of our hands and said, "I love you both." The next day when she came back there were so many tears. You see, when Jesse's mom died of cancer, Jesse and his mother had been estranged. He didn't want that to happen to me. I think that was one of his motives moving back to California—so I could reconcile with my family.

After Jesse died in 1992, all of a sudden I started becoming symptomatic. I think it had to do with the fact that I had never grieved over Jesse. The other thing that happened was when Jesse died, I realized I didn't have any other friends. We had moved here from New York and he had gotten sick almost immediately, so I didn't have a chance to establish a social network.

Then I got a job doing theater for an Asian AIDS project. I soon found out there were Asian people who had HIV but they just weren't out about it. I thought people needed to understand some of the emotional aspects of this disease. What I started to do was tell people's stories on stage. And what happened was that at the end of the play I would go up on stage and I would tell them that I am HIV positive. During one of those plays one of my actors disclosed that he's been positive. We had gone through the whole run of the play doing some pretty intense stuff and then he finally disclosed that. It brought the work we were doing to a different level.

There's this whole thing in the Asian community about keeping face, saving face. There are forty-nine different ethnicities and so many different languages, but one of the common things is keeping face. If you don't talk about certain things, you won't invite them into your house. Part of the reason is that in a lot of Asian languages there is no word for being gay. And so what they use is derogatory words.

It depends on which culture. The Chamorros are a lot more tolerant of homosexuality. In a lot of Pacific Island cultures it was actually accepted in the ancient days. But what changed was when Western missionaries came in and brought the Western Christian values and told people that they were wrong if they were homosexual.

So I have found out with my work with gay Asians that their gay identity is so much more the issue than HIV. There is a shame about that. And if you are a son, you are supposed to have a family. If you are the oldest son, you have to take care of the family name. If you are the only son, even more so. You feel like a failure when that doesn't happen.

There had been a rumor in the late '80s that Asians didn't get AIDS because you never saw anybody who had it. We were so invisible. Now there is a national network of gay Asian Pacific Islanders because HIV gave people an opportunity to look at things like identity, sexuality, and approach a lot of subjects we never talked about before.

There are people who don't identify as gay. We call them "men who have sex with men," and they're married. We need to use that label because they would never say they were gay or identify as bi [bisexual]. They are people who travel or go to anonymous sex places or may have a relationship somewhere. A lot of the time their wives are the last to know. And it's not just particular to our community. It's in the Mexican community. The drug community. There's a lot of sex that happens between men and women and men and men just because of what happens when you are an addict.

If someone walks into our Center [the Asian Pacific Wellness Center in San Francisco] and has AIDS, the disease is the smallest part of the picture. I've had clients who told me they would rather die than have their families find out they're gay. And they usually did die before they told them they had AIDS.

My biggest hope is that AIDS will change the world in a good way, that people will be able to take the losses, the vast amount of death, and that it will make a difference in the development of our people. I think it's a huge opportunity for people to learn about each other. My biggest fear is that all this pain, all this death, all this money that has been poured into fighting this disease means nothing. Another fear I have is dying before my parents, having them watch me go through what I have watched my friends go through.

My health has continued to improve. I have been on protease inhibitors. But I do get discriminated against because people perceive me as healthy. For example, at the height of illness I was given a handicapped parking placard because I couldn't control my bowels. Sometimes people would see me park and then scratch my car with keys because they thought I wasn't handicapped enough. I would have traded my AIDS diagnosis for that handicapped placard anytime.

One of the things that is happening right now is that suddenly I feel this huge connection to God. In my work I meet people who say, "Well, this is God's punishment. God doesn't love me." And I'm thinking, how could it be that God doesn't love me? God has given me the strength. God has given me the wisdom. He's given me everything I've needed to get through the last nine years. I beat the odds. I survived. God has something planned for me. I don't know what it is. He will tell me what He wants me to do and I will be glad to be doing it.

MY BIGGEST HOPE IS THAT AIDS WILL CHANGE THE WORLD IN A GOOD WAY, THAT PEOPLE WILL BE ABLE TO TAKE THE LOSSES, THE VAST AMOUNT OF DEATH, AND THAT IT WILL MAKE A DIFFERENCE IN THE DEVELOPMENT OF OUR PEOPLE. I THINK IT'S A HUGE OPPORTUNITY FOR PEOPLE TO LEARN ABOUT EACH OTHER.

Glossary

AIDS (Acquired Immunodeficiency Syndrome)

The most severe manifestation of infection by the HIV virus. AIDS destroys the body's ability to fight infection, resulting in susceptibility to many other diseases. People who are HIV positive are diagnosed as having AIDS when their T cell count is at or below 200 T cells per microliter or they have experienced a major opportunistic infection such as pneumocystis pneumonia or Kaposi's sarcoma.

The HIV virus can be transmitted through blood, semen, including pre-seminal fluid or "pre-cum," vaginal fluid, and breast milk. One can get infected by having unprotected vaginal or anal sex (without a condom), having unprotected oral sex (without a condom or other barrier), sharing needles for intravenous drug use, or sharing needles for tatooing or piercing. HIV can also be transmitted from an infected mother to her fetus or to her baby during birth or through nursing. Since 1985 in the United States all donated blood is screened for HIV.

Antiviral

A class of medications that combat HIV/AIDS. They act by destroying the virus or suppressing its replication. They are also called antiretrovirals.

AZT

Also known as zidovudine, it was the first drug approved for treating HIV disease. It is an antiretroviral.

Castro

Formerly a predominately Irish neighborhood known as Eureka Valley, the Castro is now the most gay-identified district in San Francisco. Many members of the city's gay and lesbian communities live, work, or socialize in the Castro, which has acquired a reputation throughout the world as a "gay Mecca."

Combination therapy

The use of multiple drugs or treatments against HIV/AIDS.

Detox

Shortened form of "detoxification."

Drug resistance

The ability of some infectious agents, including the HIV virus, to adapt through genetic mutation and continue multiplying in the presence of drugs that were initially effective against them.

Emancipated minor

A person under eighteen who has entered in a valid marriage or is on active duty with the armed forces, or has received a declaration of emancipation through the state. The minor willingly lives separate and apart from his or her parents or guardian. The minor has rights and responsibilities which are spelled out under the law.

GED (General Educational Development)

A program that tests academic skills and knowledge that are expected of high school graduates. By passing the High School Equivalency Diploma Test that GED offers, an individual can get a credential that is equivalent to a high school diploma.

HIV (Human Immunodeficiency Virus)

The virus that causes AIDS.

HIV-1 (Human Immunodeficiency Virus Type 1)

The virus that causes most cases of AIDS in the United States and Europe.

HIV-2 (Human Immunodeficiency Virus Type 2)

A virus closely related to HIV-1 which also causes AIDS. HIV-1 and HIV-2 have similar viral structures, modes of transmission, and opportunistic infections but predominate in different geographic regions. HIV-2 is more common in West Africa than in the United States and Europe.

Kaposi's sarcoma (KS)

A type of cancer, associated with a virus that often attacks people with a weakened immune system, including those living with HIV/AIDS. It often appears on the skin but can also affect internal organs.

Lipodystrophy

A change in the way the body produces, uses, and distributes fat. People with HIV/AIDS, particularly those who are taking antiretroviral drugs, often are affected with symptoms of lipodystrophy. These include the loss of the thin layer of fat under the skin, the wasting of the face and limbs, and the accumulation of fat on the abdomen or between the shoulder blades.

Meds

Shortened form of "medications."

Monotherapy

The use of a single drug against HIV.

Multi-Drug Rescue Therapy (MEGA-HAART)

Salvage therapy involving the use of six or more antiretroviral drugs where previous treatments have failed.

NA (Narcotics Anonymous)

An international, community-based association of recovering drug addicts, based on the twelve-step program developed by Alcoholics Anonymous.

Neuropathy

Peripheral neuropathy is nerve damage that is found in some people living with HIV/AIDS. Common symptoms include numbness, tingling, or burning in the feet or hands.

Night sweats

Extreme sweating during sleep, which is a common symptom of HIV disease.

Non-Hodgkin's lymphoma (NHL)

A cancer that starts in the lymphatic system, creating tumors. These can occur in the lymph nodes as well as throughout the body. After Kaposi's sarcoma, NHL is the most common form of cancer associated with AIDS.

Opportunistic infection

When the immune system is compromised, the body is vulnerable to a variety of illnesses, including pneumocystis pneumonia, Kaposi's sarcoma, and other parasitic viral and fungal infections.

PCP (Pneumocystis Carinii Pneumonia)

An infection of the lungs. People with AIDS whose immune systems are suppressed are vulnerable to PCP. It is a frequent cause of death in AIDS patients.

PICC (Peripherally Inserted Central Catheter) line

A long, flexible tube inserted in the neck, chest, or upper arm and threaded through the veins to the large central vein in the chest. A PICC line is used to draw blood or administer antibiotics, chemotherapy, nutrition, or transfusions where long-term intravenous treatment is required, avoiding the need for frequent venipuncture.

Protease inhibitors

Antiviral drugs that act by inhibiting the virus protease enzyme, thereby preventing replication of the virus.

Ryan White C.A.R.E. (Comprehensive AIDS Resources Emergency Care) Act

Federal legislation providing funds for health care and support services for persons living with HIV/AIDS. Named after Ryan White, a thirteen-year-old hemophiliac who was infected with HIV from a blood transfusion. He suffered discrimination and became an activist as a result. Ryan White died in 1990 at age nineteen.

Salvage therapy

Drug therapies for patients who have had a series of treatment failures. Such patients usually have few remaining treatment options.

Seroconversion

When a person who has been infected by a virus changes from testing negative for the virus to testing positive for it. This may occur even weeks or months after infection. People with HIV/AIDS have seroconverted and are called "HIV positive."

Shanti

A nonprofit organization based in San Francisco which provides services for people living with HIV/AIDS and other life-threatening illnesses. Shanti was founded in 1974 and has played an important role in San Francisco's response to AIDS.

SSI (Supplemental Security Income)

A federal income supplement program funded by general tax revenues, not Social Security taxes, which is designed to help aged, blind, and disabled people who have little or no income.

STD (Sexually transmitted disease)

A disease that can be passed from one person to another through certain sexual practices. Herpes, chlamydia, syphilus, and HIV are examples of STDs.

T cells (CD4+ T-Lymphocytes)

These white blood cells are part of the immune system and are responsible for fighting infection. The HIV virus attacks CD4 cells, killing them off. People with HIV/AIDS want their T cell count to be high. A normal T cell range is 500 to 1,500. An official diagnosis of AIDS is made when a patient's T cell count is 200 or below.

Viral load

This count measures the quantity of HIV virus in the blood. The lower the viral load, the better a patient's prognosis. Viral load testing for HIV infection is used to determine the timing, selection, and sequence of drug therapies.

ROSLYN BANISH holds a master's degree in photography from the Institute of Design in Chicago, where she studied with Aaron Siskind. She has taught photography in England, Italy, and the United States. Author of *City Families: Chicago and London* and two children's books, she lives in San Francisco.